Intervention
Annotated Teacher's Edition

Level 4

Mc Graw Hill **SRA**

Columbus, OH

SRAonline.com

 SRA

Send all inquiries to this address:
SRA/McGraw-Hill
4400 Easton Commons
Columbus, OH 43219

ISBN: 978-0-07-610428-4
MHID: 0-07-610428-1

3 4 5 6 7 8 9 COU 13 12 11 10 09 08 07

The McGraw-Hill Companies

Table of Contents

Intervention Selections

Table of Contents

Table of Contents

Grammar, Usage, and Mechanics

Table of Contents

A Snowman for Moose

by Carol Dornfeld Stevenson

Moose was sad as he looked through the window. Moose
wasn't a real moose. He was a very big dog named Moose.
Moose had an important job—to protect his friend Timmy.

Timmy was a good boy, as boys go. But he did like to wander.
Wandering was fine as long as Moose was with him. That way,
Moose could keep him out of harm's way and get him home
safely.

But today Timmy had gone out alone to play in the snow.
After building a snowman, he wandered off. And now he was
lost! A feeling of sadness came over Moose. He was not there
to protect his friend. And protection was what Moose was all
about! Moose thought about Timmy's words earlier that morning.

"You have to stay in, Moose, because you always knock
down my snowman!" He was right. Moose loved jumping up and
toppling over the snowmen that Timmy made.

Now Timmy was gone! The snowman he made was there, but   173
Timmy was nowhere in sight. And now the snow was coming   184
down more heavily than before.   189

Where was he?   192

Timmy's mother looked down the road. Timmy's father looked   201
up the road.   204

Moose slipped out. He headed for the woods, with one purpose   215
in mind—to find Timmy! Moose was sure Timmy was in the   227
woods, but Timmy wasn't there.   232

Moose then ran onto the open field. Still no sign of Timmy.   244
As Moose slowly plodded on, he could almost see the old barn at   257
the far edge of the field. Maybe Timmy was there, taking shelter   269
from the snowstorm.   272

There he was!   275

Moose jumped up and down, wagging his tail and barking   285
happily. Timmy was safe! Moose led him home through the   295
snow.   296

"I lost my way in the snow," Timmy explained to his parents,   308
"but Moose found me!   312

"Let's celebrate!" cried Timmy's mother. And what a   320
celebration it was. Moose got more treats in one afternoon than   331
he had gotten all week! And his best treat was still to come.   344

By the next morning, the snow had stopped. Timmy's   353
snowman was still standing in the yard.   360

"Come on, Moose!" Timmy yelled. "Let's go out and topple   370
over the snowman!"   373

The Girl with Golden Hair

retold by Lynn Samuel

5

9

21

32

44

56

68

76

87

89

100

Long ago, people did not know how to grow crops. In the spring and summer, they ate roots, bark, nuts, and leaves. When winter arrived, they had nothing to eat. It was a difficult life!

One spring day, an old man slept under a tree. He awoke suddenly to the sound of someone singing. At the edge of the woods, he saw a girl with golden hair.

"If you follow my instruction, you will never go hungry again," she said.

"I will gladly do as you say," replied the old man.

"Then take this lock of my golden hair to the field and brush it over the ground. A new corn plant will quickly spring up wherever my hair touches," she said. "The plant will grow very tall, and by the end of the summer, you will have many plants to harvest. They will feed you and your people throughout the winter. But keep some of the seeds to plant next spring."

113

125

136

149

160

171

And with that, the girl disappeared. 177

The man did as he was told. He truly believed that if he 190
followed the girl's instruction, he would have enough food for 200
himself and his people. 204

Soon after the old man brushed the field with the girl's hair, 216
tiny plants began to sprout. As they grew tall, the bright reflection 228
of the sun's rays on the silk of the corn reminded the old man of 243
the girl with the golden hair. 249

The old man harvested the corn, cooked it, and shared it with 261
his people. All winter, they had corn to eat. The next spring, the 274
old man and his people planted the seeds. Again, the corn plants 286
grew tall. They would never go hungry again. 294

A Peaceful Warrior

by Joan Dalin

Martin Luther King, Jr. was born on January 15, 1929,   16
in Atlanta, Georgia. He fought for Americans' rights using   25
non-violent forms of protest. King was also a preacher.   35
Preaching taught him how to inspire people.   42

Changing the Laws   45

Before the 1960s, unfair laws were enforced in the American   55
South. Life was difficult for African Americans because they   64
were considered unequal under the law. Martin Luther King,   73
Jr. resolved to fight for equal rights for African Americans as a   85
peaceful protestor. He used boycotts to protest discrimination.   93
When many people refuse to use something, they participate in   103
a boycott. From 1955 to 1956, King led a boycott of all buses in   117
Montgomery, Alabama.   119

For one year, African Americans refused to ride buses. They   129
wanted the right to sit anywhere on the bus, just like white   141
people. The boycott worked! On December 21, 1956, African   150
Americans and whites finally rode the Montgomery buses side   159
by side.   161

Peaceful Protests Work

King also used sit-ins to peacefully protest discrimination. 173
During sit-ins, African Americans sat quietly in places marked 183
"for whites only," such as lunch counters and libraries. King was 194
arrested during a sit-in but was released. Sit-ins influenced new 206
laws that changed the "whites only" rule in many places. 216

In 1963, King held many non-violent demonstrations in 225
Birmingham, Alabama. The demonstrations protested "whites 231
only" public property. King and other demonstrators were 239
arrested. However, the demonstrations worked. The Supreme 246
Court ruled that Birmingham's "whites only" rules were 254
unconstitutional. 255

In 1963, the governor of Alabama stopped two African 264
American students from registering for classes at the University 273
of Alabama. In response, King led a march in Washington, D.C. 284
Two hundred and fifty thousand people of all races walked 294
together through the nation's capital. Then King gave his famous 304
speech: "I Have a Dream." 309

In April of 1968, King was shot and killed in Memphis, 320
Tennessee. King fought for the rights of all Americans until his 331
death. He was a true American hero. 338

Rosa Parks Makes History

by Duncan Searl

Rosa Parks is Arrested

On December 1, 1955, Rosa Parks boarded a bus for home after work. Little did she know her ride would go down in history.

At the next stop, some white riders boarded. One man had to stand. "Hey!" the bus driver called to Rosa. "Give the man your seat!" On the segregated buses of Montgomery, Alabama, white riders got seats first.

Rosa Parks did not move.

"Make it right for yourself. Just give him the seat," the driver ordered.

The driver's yell did not disturb Rosa Parks. She stayed put. Giving in wouldn't "make it right" for her. The more African Americans in Alabama gave in, the worse they were treated.

"I'll have you arrested," the driver warned.

"You may do that," Rose Parks replied gently.

At the next stop, two policemen zipped Rosa Parks off to the city jail.

African Americans Protest

News of the arrest spread, and African Americans got angry. They had had enough of segregation. Lawyers persuaded Rosa Parks to become a test case. They wanted to prove that bus segregation was unfair and illegal. The case went all the way to the U.S. Supreme Court.

African Americans boycotted the buses. They formed carpools, took cabs, rode bikes, and walked; they did not ride the buses. A young minister in Montgomery led the boycott. His name was Martin Luther King, Jr.

Without African American riders, the bus company lost money. So did businessmen along the bus routes. They tried to stop the boycott, but African Americans stood firm. Month in, month out, they didn't ride the buses.

Segregated Buses Are Declared Illegal

After a year of review, news came from Washington. The Supreme Court justices agreed with Rosa Parks that segregated buses were illegal. All citizens have the right to be treated equally when riding buses.

The rest is history. The Civil Rights Movement had begun. Rosa Parks' case was the start of it all!

Intervention

Sarah and the Appaloosas

by Olivia Berkart

In 1887, I lived on a farm in Idaho with my parents and sister 21
Sarah. The land was so beautiful and rich. We grew strawberries 32
as big as apples! 36

One day, Sarah and I went fishing. We saw a young Native 48
American boy nearby. He was from the Nez Perce ('nez-'pərs) 59
tribe. We knew that a few weeks earlier the Army was escorting 71
the Nez Perce to the reservation at Lapwai when a battle broke 83
out. The Nez Perce escaped and were determined to return to 94
their homeland. 96

My sister and I walked over to the boy and introduced 107
ourselves to him. He said his name was Wolf Dog, and his people 120
had been running from the Army since the battle. They were 131
tired and sad but would keep running to keep their freedom. 142

The day before, the soldiers captured the Nez Perce and 152
their horses. The Nez Perce bred horses called Appaloosas. The 162
horses were fast, strong, and smart. Without horses, the Nez 172
Perce could not escape. Without the Appaloosas, Wolf Dog's 181
people couldn't return home. 185

Sarah said the Army was wrong to take the Appaloosas from the Nez Perce. She wanted to free the horses. I didn't think we could stop the Army, but Sarah said we needed to try. Then I got an idea. 196 209 223 225

Over one hundred Appaloosas were corralled near town. There was a traveling circus camped there, too. The circus was showing one of the first motorcars ever built. People would pay a nickel to see someone drive it around. I knew that this car would free the Appaloosas. 233 244 255 268 272

I snuck into the circus tent and found the car. I got in and started it. It was so noisy! The soldiers came from all over town to see the car. The horses were left unguarded. They didn't hear Sarah and Wolf Dog free the horses until it was too late! The Nez Perce could escape! 286 299 311 325 328

Intervention

Jo

by Tara McCarthy

When we were younger, my sister Sam had a difficult time
making friends. She was very shy. One day Sam told me she had
a new friend named Jo. But Jo was an imaginary character from
her favorite book.

"You need *real* friends," I said to Sam, "not imaginary ones."

"But Jo *is* real!" Sam said. "I have so much fun with her. She
was a pioneer over a hundred years ago. She always wears a
dress and a bonnet on her head."

"If she lived long ago, how can you see her now?" I asked.

"I don't know, but she is a good friend. We play in the
backyard."

Sam was little then. Since I was her big brother, I took good
care of her. I wanted her to have real friends, so we went to the
playground to meet other children.

15
28
40
43

54

68
80
87

100

113
114

127
142
147

"Meet May and Ben," I said. "You should play with them." 158

"Can Jo play, too?" asked Sam. 164

May and Ben looked around. "Who's Jo?" they asked. 173

I was getting annoyed, so we left the park. 182

At home I said, "Sam, no one else can see or play with Jo. She 197
isn't real." 199

Sam always counted on me for the truth. 207

"Okay," she said sadly, "I'll tell Jo I can't play with her 219
anymore. I guess it's time I made new friends." 228

The next day Sam played with May and Ben. Sam said 239
nothing about Jo, and I was happy to see her playing with new 252
friends. 253

I felt so great that night! Sam was growing up! Suddenly I 265
heard a strange voice in the backyard. I looked out the window. 277
A girl wearing a dress and a bonnet stood outside. It was Jo! 290

"You're a good brother," she said quietly. "You helped Sam 300
make new friends." Then Jo disappeared. 306

I wasn't the only one to help Sam. Jo was Sam's friend, too, 319
when she really needed one. 324

Intervention

No Pets Allowed!

by Kathy Wong

Mrs. Crocker wanted a pet to keep her company. 15
Unfortunately, the landlord, Mr. Glumly, put signs everywhere in 24
the apartment building: No Pets Allowed! 30

"How about one bird?" Mrs. Crocker asked Mr. Glumly. 39

"No pets means no pets!" Mr. Glumly said. "If you have one 51
bird, someone else will want three!" 57

"How about a turtle?" asked Mrs. Crocker. 64

"No pets allowed!" said Mr. Glumly. 70

One morning Mrs. Crocker saw this ad in the newspaper: *The* 81
Lucky Animal Shelter needs your help! Be kind to animals at 92
the shelter. Walk the dogs, pet the cats. Sign up today! 103

"Sounds great!" thought Mrs. Crocker. She signed up at the 113
shelter. She walked a dog named Penny and petted ten cats. 124
A puppy licked her face. But Mrs. Crocker couldn't play with all 136
of the dogs and cats. They needed more funds and volunteers. 147
Mrs. Crocker wanted to do more. 153

When she got home, she saw Mr. Glumly. 161

"Guess what!" Mrs. Crocker said to him. "I have a dog and six 174
kittens." 175

Mr. Glumly looked into the apartment. He didn't see any pets. 186
"Very funny!" he said. 190

Mrs. Crocker's neighbor said she was lonely and wanted a 200
pet, too. Mrs. Crocker brought her to the shelter the next day. 212

The workers at the shelter wondered how they would find 222
homes for all of the animals. 228

"No problem!" said Mrs. Crocker. "I'll call some of my 238
neighbors. I'll tell them about the shelter." Mrs. Crocker 247
found more volunteers. She saw Mr. Howell at the market. He 258
suggested a fundraiser at his store. They could raise money and 269
find homes for the animals. 274

Mrs. Crocker helped the shelter organize the fundraiser. 282
She took pictures of the dogs and cats that needed homes. The 294
fundraiser was a success! The shelter found homes for many 305
animals and raised a lot of money. 312

Mrs. Crocker felt happy. Now she had many pets to play with 324
and keep her company. 328

The New Mitt

by Kit Murphy

Lovida loved softball. "I'm going to be a pitcher," she told Ted. "One day, I'll be a famous ballplayer." 18 25

Ted was Lovida's next-door neighbor. Ted loved to play ball, too. "I'm a home-run hitter," said Ted. "Watch me knock the ball out of the park." 36 49 53

Ted had a new, red mitt. He had earned the money to buy it. He walked Mrs. Miller's dog. 67 72

Lovida wanted a new mitt, too. But she didn't have enough money. 83 84

"You can earn the money," said Ted. "Mrs. Green needs someone to walk her dog." 94 99

"But then I can't play ball," said Lovida. "Softball is fun. Walking dogs is boring." 110 114

One afternoon, Lovida went to get Ted. "Come on, Ted. Let's play ball," she called. 125 129

"I can't," answered Ted. "I'm walking dogs today. I'm earning money for a bat." 139 143

"Well, I want to play," said Lovida. "Let me borrow your new mitt." 154
156

"It looks like rain," said Ted. "I don't want it to get wet." 169

"Don't worry. Nothing will happen to it," promised Lovida. 178

Later, it began to rain. A crash of thunder frightened Lovida. She ran home in a hurry. She left Ted's mitt at the ballpark. 189
202

The mitt was ruined. It was wet and dirty. Ted was upset. 214

"I'm sorry," said Lovida. "How can I get you a new mitt? I don't have any money." 226
231

"You could walk dogs," said Ted. 237

"Then when will I play ball?" asked Lovida. 245

"We can play catch with the dogs," said Ted. 254

"That's a great idea," said Lovida. "We can earn money and play ball at the same time. I can buy you another mitt. And maybe I can get one for myself, too." 265
268
276

Li Chi and the Mermaid

by June Bodansky

Li Chi lived with her mother, her father, and her dog, Tiny, in a small house between a mountain and a lake. The sea was also nearby.

Every morning, Li Chi watched the sunrise over the lake. One morning she heard someone cry out.

"Please help me!" cried a woman swimming in the lake.

"Who are you?" Li Chi asked.

"My name is Kai. I'm a mermaid. I am part woman and part fish. I live in the sea." she said.

"Why are you in the lake?" Li Chi asked.

"I got lost. I swam into a cave that led into the lake. The lake is angry because I swam in it. I can't get out, but you can help me get home."

"How?"

"A white rose grows on the mountain. Fetch it and throw it into the lake. Then the lake will let me go. The sea is angry, too. It will flood the lake and wreck your house if I am not back tomorrow."

Li Chi told her parents about the mermaid.

"We must find the rose," said Father. "We have to help the mermaid and save our home."

"Father," Li Chi said, "it's getting dark. We won't be able to see. A trip to the mountain will be dangerous!"

"We must take the risk," said Mother. "We cannot wait."

They climbed the steep mountain. At last they reached the   250
top. Where was the rose? They searched and searched but did   261
not find it.   264

Then Tiny started barking near a stone. Li Chi ran to the   276
stone and saw a white rose growing behind it. She cried with joy 289
as she carefully picked the rose.   295

Slowly they climbed back down the mountain. It was so dark!   306
Li Chi raced to the lake and tossed in the rose. Kai was finally 320
free to swim home. She waved good-bye as she swam away.   332

"We took a great risk, but now we are safe!" cried Mother.   344

The Woodsman and the Ax

by Rosalie Koskenmaki

5

8

Long ago, in a deep forest a man sat on a rock near a small pool weeping. He was a poor man and not well-dressed. His hands looked rough; he surely knew hard work. As he sat there on the rock, he felt sad and tired.

"Why do you weep?" asked a voice.

The man looked up. A tall stranger stood in front of him. He was dressed in fine silk clothes. He had a very kind face.

The weeping man spoke. "I am a poor woodsman. I lost my ax and can do no work. My wife and children will starve."

The stranger softly spoke a single word. A beautiful golden ax rose from the pool. "Is this your ax?" the stranger asked.

"Oh, no. I'm sorry to say that is not my ax," the woodsman answered.

23
35
47
55

62

75
87

99
111

121
133

146
147

The stranger said the word again. This time, a silver ax   158
appeared. "Is *this* your ax?"   163

The woodsman answered sadly, "No, but thank you for your   173
trouble."   174

Then the stranger brought up the woodsman's own ax. "Yes!"   184
he cried. "That's it!"   188

The stranger smiled and said, "Keep all three axes." He sent   199
the woodsman off, singing joyfully.   204

A man who lived nearby heard the story. He wanted the same   216
good luck, so he went and sat by the pool. Soon he threw his ax   231
into the pool and wept loudly. The stranger appeared. The man   242
heard a gentle voice and saw a tall stranger standing in front of   255
him. The stranger asked why the man was weeping. The man   266
told him that he had lost his ax. It had fallen into the pool.   280

The stranger brought up a golden ax. "Is this your ax?"   291

The man cried, "Yes! That is my ax!"   299

Hearing this, the stranger threw the gold ax back into the   310
pool. He drove the man away. Now the man cried real tears,   322
for he had no ax at all!   329

An Underwater Doctor's Office

by Elizabeth Ann Hamilton

"Next, please!"

When you watch what is going on for a while, you can almost hear those words. The doctor seems to be asking the patient to come into his office. But no one says a word. They can't. Both the "doctor" and the "patient" are fish.

A small fish, called a wrasse, acts like a doctor. Some wrasses are found in waters around coral reefs. Coral reefs are full of life. Some of the plants and animals living there are very tiny. In fact, they are small enough to live on the skin of other fish! But if too many of them live on a single fish, that fish becomes sick. It may even die.

The wrasse helps keep fish healthy. It eats the tiny plants and animals growing on the fish and cleans their skin. The fish feel better, and the wrasse gets a free meal!

The fish that come for cleaning are much bigger than the wrasse. Most big fish like to eat smaller fish, but they never hurt the wrasse. Instead, they remain very still. The "doctor" nibbles on the plants and animals on their skin with small, sharp teeth. The wrasse can even swim into their mouths, and it will still be safe!

Doctors sometimes wear uniforms. The wrasse has a uniform, too. Its body is marked with bright blue and black bars. Most fish are camouflaged to hide from other fish. The wrasse, however, wants to be seen. It will even swim in front of a big fish and do a dance! It seems to say, "Let me help you feel better!"

Fish don't need to be told about the wrasse. They know there   288
is a certain place on the reef to get help. When their skin starts to   303
bother them, they swim to that spot. If the wrasse is busy, they   316
wait. A diver once saw one small wrasse care for three hundred   328
fish in six hours! This little "doctor" is certainly important to the   340
life of the reef!   344

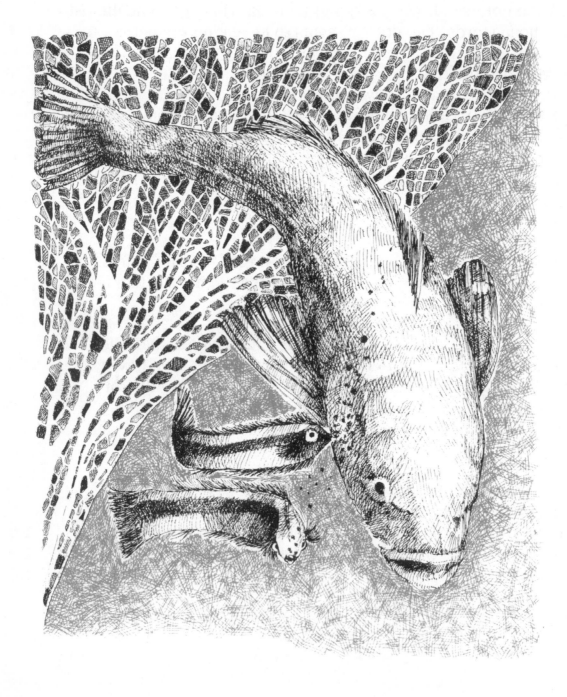

The Water We All Share

by Travis Harper

Where do you get water? From a faucet, right? In fact, water travels a long way before reaching the faucet. Water is always on the move: in the sky, below the ground, or in a river. Even the water you drink stays in your body for just a short time.

Water reaches your home through buried pipes. The pipes are filled miles away at a water treatment plant. Most plants get their water from large lakes or rivers.

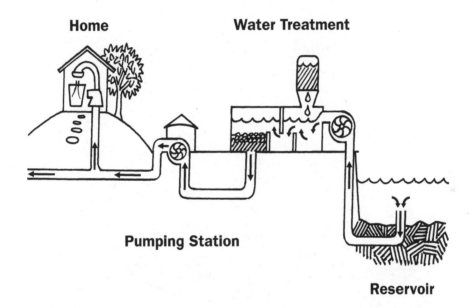

Home

Water Treatment

Pumping Station

Reservoir

At the treatment plant, dirt is removed from the water. The water is run through sand and gravel filters. Next, chemicals are added to kill bacteria that might make you sick. Then the water is pumped to your home.

After you use the water, it flows to a sewage plant. Large pieces of solid waste are filtered out first. Then the water sits for a while in giant tanks. Any solids that remain sink to the bottom. At the same time, grease and other fats rise and are skimmed from the top.

5
8
20
31
46
58
67
79
86
97
108
120
125
137
150
163
175
178

The water is treated again with chemicals and sent back into   189
nature. This water must be clean! Dirty water hurts living things. 200
The next town downstream needs the water for its treatment   210
plants.   211

After a while, much of the water we use reaches the ocean.   223
Some of it, though, ends up in the sky. Lakes, ponds, and   235
even puddles send water into the air. It evaporates from their   246
surfaces. That means it changes from a liquid to a gas.   257

Water that collects in the sky forms clouds. As the wind   268
blows, the clouds carry the water to new places. It returns to   280
land as rain, hail, sleet, or snow. Then the water flows back into 293
creeks, rivers, and sewers. The water treatment cycle begins   302
again.   303

Think about the water you drink today. It might contain some   314
of the same water you drank a week ago!   323

Nature's Balance

by Marianne Conrad

    Have you ever built a tower with cards? You must balance
every card in just the right place. A little push will upset the
balance and make the tower fall. The air around the earth has a
delicate balance, too.

    Air is made up of many gases. Two of these gases are oxygen
and carbon dioxide. Humans and animals inhale oxygen and
exhale carbon dioxide. Plants do just the opposite. They inhale
carbon dioxide and exhale oxygen. Animals and plants work
together to balance the gases in the air.

This balance is important. When the gases in the air are 100
balanced, they maintain the temperature of the earth. Energy 109
from the sun goes through the air and strikes the earth. Some 121
energy bounces back and is trapped in the air as heat. Without 133
air, the earth would be very cold. The balance of gases keeps the 146
earth's temperature steady. 149

When people burn coal or oil, carbon dioxide goes into the 160
air. This extra carbon dioxide absorbs more heat energy from 170
Earth and makes the earth hotter. We call this global warming. 181
Global warming could cause the ice at the North and South 192
Poles to melt. Then the water level of the oceans would rise. 204
Land near the oceans would be under water! 212

Some rays from the sun can cause health problems for 222
humans. Ozone, another gas in the air, protects the earth from 233
harmful rays. But gases that escape from spray cans and 243
refrigerators rise in the air and destroy ozone. Eventually, there 253
might not be enough ozone to block the sun's harmful rays. 264

What can you do to help balance nature's gases? Plant trees 275
as often as you can. Avoid using spray containers that release 286
harmful gases. Remember that you can help care for the air 297
around the earth. We can all help to protect the beautiful world 309
around us. 311

A Little Shocking

by Jennifer Ramos

Brrrrring! The alarm goes off, and you roll out of bed. It's a   19
dark, cold winter morning. You shuffle across the carpet to turn   30
on the light. Just as your fingers get close to the wall—SNAP!   43
You see a tiny burst of light and feel a pinch of pain. You're wide   58
awake now, thanks to static electricity!   64

    Why did you get shocked? The answer starts with atoms. They   75
are the building blocks of our world. Atoms make up everything.   86
Your body, the carpet, and even the air are made of atoms.   98

    There are three things inside an atom: electrons, protons,   107
and neutrons. Protons and neutrons are packed into the atom's   117
center, called the nucleus (new clee us). Electrons fly around the   128
nucleus like the planets going around the sun.   136

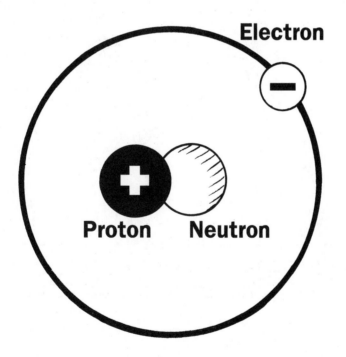

Electron

Proton   **Neutron**

    Atoms want the same number of electrons and protons.   145
They like to be balanced. Electrons can jump from one atom to   157
another, though. Some atoms easily lose electrons. Others gain   166
them. This means that an atom can sometimes have unequal   176
numbers of electrons and protons. These unbalanced atoms look   185
for ways to be balanced again.   191

When objects touch each other, their atoms trade some   200
electrons. If they are rubbed together, even more electrons are 210
traded. Feet rubbed across carpet pick up lots of electrons. The 221
extra electrons jump from atom to atom in your body. They are   233
looking for a place to go.   239

Water likes to take on extra electrons. During summer, the air   250
has more moisture in it. Your body's extra electrons pass quickly 261
into the humid air. During winter, though, the air is dry. Instead, 273
your body's atoms wait for you to get near an object that wants   286
electrons. Then the extra electrons rush out in one big burst.   297
That's static electricity. Shocking!   301

Now the atoms in your body are balanced again. It's time to   313
shuffle across the ground and pick up more electrons. Next time 324
you "zap" a friend, explain what happened. Then he or she might 336
not be so mad!   340

Food Chain

by Benito Agosto

A tree grows tall in the forest. Its branches reach out, and its
leaves soak up the sunlight. Its roots sink deep into the ground
to drink up water and nutrients. The tree uses these things to
make energy. Then it uses that energy to grow even taller.

A snail sits on a leaf and sticks out its rough tongue. The
snail scrapes up bits of the leaf. It eats the leaf to get the food
it needs. Later, a mouse sees the snail in a garden. The mouse
darts over and gulps down the snail. The snail becomes the food
the mouse needs.

A snake spies the mouse as it sleeps. The snake slides near. It
opens its mouth wide and swallows the mouse whole. The snake
eats the mouse for food. Later, a red-tailed hawk waits on its
perch. It sees the snake and swoops down, catches it, and eats it.
The snake is the food the hawk needs.

18
30
42
53

66
81
94
106
109

122
133
146
159
167

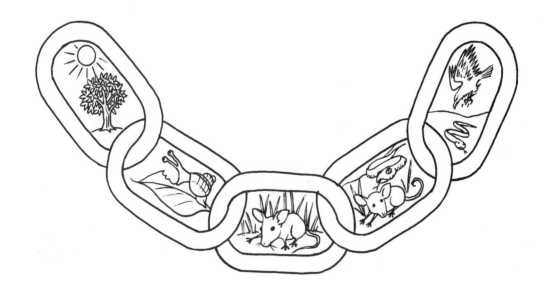

All living things need food. The foods they eat are like the   179
links in a chain. The first link in this food chain is the leaf,   193
and the last link is the hawk. All food chains start with plants.   206
Plants make their own food. They use soil, air, water, and light   218
from the sun.   221

Animals that eat just plants come next in the chain. They are   233
called herbivores. They eat plants and fruits from plants. This   243
includes grass, seeds, nuts, and berries.   249

Animals that eat other animals come next in the chain. They   260
are called carnivores. They eat meat. Their sharp claws, teeth,   270
and beaks help with this task.   276

Some animals eat both plants and meat. They are called   286
omnivores. Their place in a food chain changes depending on   296
what they eat—and what eats them.   303

When a plant or animal dies, it starts to rot. Nutrients sink   315
into the soil. The soil helps new plants grow. Then another food   327
chain begins again!   330

Nature's Pressure Cooker

by Anthony Wallace

|---|---|
| | 3 |
| | 6 |

Nothing is harder than rock, right? Deep within Earth, though, rock is melting. High temperatures and pressure change rock into a liquid. An ocean of this liquid, called magma, flows about fifty miles underground. When magma rises to Earth's surface, it is called lava. Sometimes lava just oozes. Other times, it erupts forcefully. A few things determine which will happen. `15 24 36 45 56 66`

Earth's surface, or crust, is broken into giant parts, called plates. They come in many shapes and sizes. The plates float on top of the layer of magma. We can't feel it, but the plates move about two inches each year. As the plates bump into one another, pressure builds. When the pressure becomes too great, an earthquake happens. This releases the pressure between the plates, at least for a little while. `76 87 101 113 122 131 138`

Earth's plates don't fit tightly together. The seams are full of cracks and openings. Most volcanoes form at one of these seams. The pressure between two plates pushes magma upward. The magma moves through an opening called a vent. Vents can be wide or narrow. Some magma is a thin liquid, like milk. It easily oozes to the surface, flows out of the vent, cools, and hardens. As this happens over and over, the layers of lava eventually form a mountain. This mountain is called a volcano. If the lava keeps flowing, the volcano is less likely to erupt. `148 159 168 179 192 204 215 225 237`

Some magma is thick like a milkshake. It doesn't flow easily through the vent. A narrow vent makes the problem even worse. Pressure from the moving plates keeps building. It isn't being released quickly enough through the vent. `248 259 269 275`

When the pressure is too strong, the volcano erupts. Lava, 285
ash, and rock fly into the air. Debris can travel for hundreds of 298
miles. Once the pressure is released, the volcano quiets down. 308
Lava keeps flowing, though. It hardens, and the volcano rebuilds 318
itself. Pressure deep inside Earth begins growing again too. The 328
whole process is about to restart. 334

Good Garbage

by Victoria Sung

What did you have for dinner last night? Were there leftovers? 16
Even if you ate most of your meal, some food probably ended up 29
in the trash. Many people recycle cans, plastic, and glass. When 40
you create a compost pile, you can reuse all kinds of natural 52
things, too. 54

All you need to begin your compost pile is some space outside. 66
Most people put their piles near the garden. Grass clippings or 77
old leaves make a good first layer. If you have small twigs, place 90
them on the bottom. They will keep the air flowing. 100

Now add kitchen waste. Potato peels, rotten berries, and 109
bits of beans are all food waste. Add old coffee grounds and 121
eggshells. Even hair clippings from a home haircut can be 131
useful. Don't add meat, bones, cheese, or fats. These things 141
attract animals! You don't want a yard full of critters digging 152
through your compost! 155

Mix new scraps in with a rake to blend fresh items with   167
rotting ones. Water the compost often, but don't make it too wet.   179
It should feel like a damp sponge. Compost piles that work the   191
fastest have a mix of two elements called nitrogen and carbon.   202
Most of your scraps will contain these elements.   210

Nature is good at recycling. It will do the rest of the work.   223
As the mix rots, it heats up. The center of the pile can reach 150   238
degrees! The heat comes from tiny bacteria that decompose, or   248
break down, the material. Lots of other creatures, like worms,   258
snails, and ants, do the same kind of work. Once the compost   270
cools, the cycle is done.   275

When it's ready, the compost will be dark and crumbly. It   286
won't smell like garbage. Instead it will have a rich, earthy scent.   298
All the nutrients that were in the waste you added to the bin are   312
still there. They will help you grow your own potatoes, berries,   323
or beans. Save the peels, stems, and leftovers, though! Put them   334
back into the bin to start the compost for next year's garden.   346

By the Light of the Moon

by Satish Reddy

The moon has always been important to humans. Long before
it was understood, people made up stories, songs, and poems
about the moon. The moon was lovely but mysterious.

Today we understand why it always looks different. The
moon doesn't change, but the view from Earth does. The moon
doesn't give off its own light. It reflects sunlight off its surface.
When the lit side faces Earth, the moon can be seen.

The moon moves around Earth in a circle called an orbit.
One orbit takes about twenty-seven days. When the moon is in
different places, our view of it changes. These different views
are called phases. A new moon occurs when the sun and the
moon are on the same side of Earth. The sun shines on the side
of the moon that faces away from Earth. A new moon looks
black. It blends into the night sky, so it's hard to see.

92
104
114
126
140
152
164

A full moon occurs when the sun and moon are on opposite 176
sides of Earth. The side of the moon facing Earth is brightly 188
lit. There are many names for a full moon. In the fall it's called 202
the harvest moon. When do you think the snow moon or the 214
planter's moon appear? 217

When the moon changes from full to new, it is waning, or 229
getting smaller. When it changes from new to full, it is waxing, 241
or getting larger. Of course, it's not really changing size. It just 253
looks that way. 256

When only a sliver of the moon can be seen, it is called a 270
crescent moon. Have you ever eaten a crescent-shaped roll, or 281
a croissant? If you have, you know what a crescent moon looks 293
like. It can be seen during both the waxing and waning phases. 305

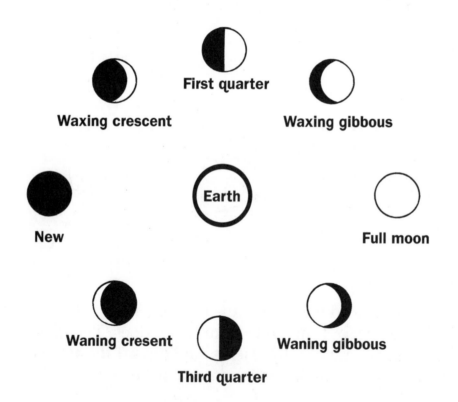

On the next clear night, walk outside and see if you can spot 318
the moon. Can you tell which phase it is in? Try again a week 332
later. Were you right? Though the moon may not be mysterious 343
anymore, it is still lovely! 348

The Great Sequoia Trees

by Maria Handelman

Sequoias are the largest trees in the world. They are named in honor of Sequoia, the great Cherokee leader and inventor of the Cherokee written language.

Sequoia trees grow between 250 and 300 feet tall. The largest one, named General Sherman, is 272 feet tall, more than 100 feet around, and still growing! General Sherman weighs about 4,000 tons and is big enough to build 40 five-room houses! The sequoias are the tallest and *oldest* trees in the world. The oldest living sequoia is 3,300 years old!

New sequoias sprout from tiny seeds. They are tucked away inside cones that hang off the branches. For new trees to grow, seeds must be released from the cones. This happens when squirrels or beetles pick at the cones. However, fire does the best job of releasing seeds.

When fire strikes, heat from the flames dries the cones. The   154
cones open and drop seeds onto the forest floor. When logs on   166
the ground are burned, ash is left behind. The tiny seeds grow   178
best in this ash.   182

Every year 500,000 sequoia seeds are spread on forest floors,   192
but only a handful of those seed will germinate, or start to grow.   205
If the conditions are just right, the seed swells and cracks open.   217
A root reaches down into the soil, and a stem grows up toward   230
the light. After a few days, the new sequoia looks like a short   243
blade of grass. Once the sapling is strong, it can grow up to two   257
feet each year. Sequoia trees can grow rapidly because their   267
wood and bark contain chemicals that fight disease and insects   277
better than other trees.   281

One of the most popular places to see these trees is Sequoia   293
and Kings Canyon National Park in west central California. This   303
is the park where General Sherman lives along with slightly   313
shorter sequoias named General Grant and the Washington   321
Trees. For over 100 years, millions of people have visited this   332
national park to see the Great Sequoias.   339

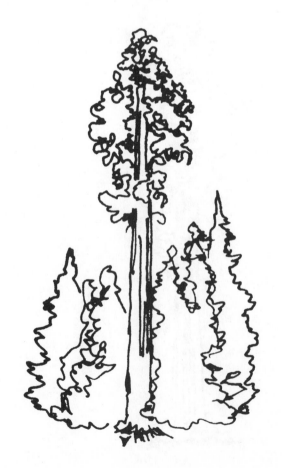

The Year of a Tree

by Maria Gomez

The limbs of the trees are bare, but small buds of leaves and flowers are just starting to emerge. Spring has arrived! A tree knows when it's time to wake up and start growing again. It feels the weather getting warmer and the days getting longer. Some trees' buds produce flowers first. The whole tree looks like a giant bouquet. Pollen, which helps trees make seeds, is released from each flower. The wind blows through the flowers, picks up pollen, and carries it to other trees. Birds and insects are drawn to drink the sweet nectar in the flowers. When a creature digs for nectar, it also gets pollen on its body. Then it spreads the pollen as it flies from tree to tree.

After the flowers have done their job, it's time for the leaves to come out. A leaf is an organ for the tree. Like your heart and lungs, leaves perform a task that helps the tree live. They absorb sunlight. A leaf's flat, thin shape is perfect for this job. Light is used to make the tree's food.

Each leaf is filled with a chemical called chlorophyll (klōr' ə   200
fil). Chlorophyll makes leaves green. It's also what causes the   210
leaves to soak up so much sunlight. The light mixes with water   222
and carbon dioxide inside the leaf. This gives the tree energy   233
to grow. As trees make food from sunlight, they also create   244
oxygen. They don't need it, so the leaves give it away. Trees are   257
very important for life on our planet!   264

As fall arrives, the days become shorter. The weather cools.   274
The tree knows winter is on its way. In cold months, there is   287
not enough water or sunlight to keep the leaves filled with   298
chlorophyll. They lose their green color and fall off. If the leaves   310
aren't making food, the trees don't need them.   318

Soon the tree's branches stand bare against a gray sky again.   329
They wait patiently for warmer weather. When they wake up,   339
the cycle begins again.   343

The First American Settlers

by Maria Diaz

Native peoples lived in North America long before Europeans.
Scientists believe these people came from Asia thousands of
years ago. At the time, much of the earth that is now under
water was dry land. People may have walked across land that
joined Asia and North America. Today water covers that land.

Many Peoples, Many Ways

There were many different groups, or tribes, of Native
Americans. Each group spoke separate languages and had
unique ways of life. Some lived in villages, while others moved
all year, hunting animals and picking wild plants. Some lived
in cities. The Aztec and Maya of Central America lived in large
cities with as many as 100,000 people. In eastern North America,
Native Americans lived in small villages and farmed. They
grew corn, beans, and squash. In South America, the Native
Americans lived in small groups and ate mainly fish and berries.

The Spanish Arrive

Around 1500, the Spanish arrived in North America. At first, the
Native Americans and the Spanish were friendly to each other.
The Native Americans taught the Spanish how to survive. They
showed them how to travel by canoe and offered them new
foods, like peanuts, corn, and tomatoes. In return, the Spanish
gave the Native Americans metal tools, cattle, and horses.

Then things began to change. The Spanish and the Native 228
Americans had different ways of life. They didn't understand 237
each other's ways of doing things. The Spanish also wanted the 248
lands and riches for themselves. Soon the Spanish and Native 258
Americans were fighting. 261

Fighting continued as the English, the Dutch, and other 270
Europeans came to North America. When the Europeans finally 279
made peace with the Native Americans, millions of Native 288
Americans had died from disease and war. Others had lost all 299
their lands. 301

Language, Culture, and Tradition 305

The Native Americans deserve our thanks. Over half our states 315
have Native American names. Hundreds of mountains, rivers, 323
and cities do, too. We use many Native American words, like 334
canoe, toboggan, and *skunk.* We eat peanuts, squash, and corn. 344
Native Americans first grew these foods. Most important of 353
all, we are learning to respect and protect nature, too. It is 365
important to honor and remember the first Americans. 373

The Third Doll

by David Downard

Sarah roamed about the woods near her new home in
Plymouth Colony. Her family had arrived on the ship *Mayflower*
just one week earlier. She was still adjusting to her new
surroundings. Plymouth was so different from her hometown
in England.

Suddenly, Sarah heard a noise that sounded like a voice. She
saw a Native American boy about her own age appear from
behind a tall mound of dirt. He approached Sarah and spoke
a few words aloud to her, but Sarah could not understand his
language.

Sarah noticed that the boy was holding something in his
hand. Initially, she thought it was a toy. When the boy came
nearer, she realized he was holding a doll of some kind. The
boy sat down on the ground and held out the doll to Sarah. She
joined him on the ground and took the doll. It was crafted from
a whole dried apple! Apple seeds had been inserted for the doll's
eyes, mouth, and ears. How cleverly it was made!

16
26
37
45
47

58
69
80
92
93

103
115
127
141
154
166
175

Quickly, Sarah arose and ran to her house. She returned a   186
minute later, proudly holding a doll of her own. She handed   197
it to the boy, who clearly enjoyed how it looked. Sarah's doll   209
had been made from an old white sock with a small amount of   222
cotton stuffing inside. Sarah had painted the face to look like   233
a clown.   235

Without speaking a word, Sarah and the Native American boy   245
played together with the dolls. After a while, Sarah ran back   256
to her house and returned shortly with another sock, not yet   267
painted. The boy immediately took another dried apple from the   277
bag he carried. This one had not yet been made into a doll.   290

Together in silence, Sarah and the boy began to make a third   302
doll. They placed the sock over the apple. Then they designed   313
the face with paint and apple seeds. After an hour the doll was   326
complete, and Sarah knew she had found her first new friend   337
in Plymouth.   339

William Penn: Father of Pennsylvania

by Zach Cantrell

William Penn was born in England in 1644. He was the son of a naval officer named Admiral Sir William Penn. The younger Penn attended a university in England in 1660, but he had trouble adjusting to the religious rules of the school. Finally, he left the university to travel and study in other countries. After two years of travel, Penn's father sent him to study law in London.

Move to America

King Charles II owed Penn's father a debt. To repay the Penn family, the King set up a colony in America for the younger Penn. In 1681, a charter gave William the territory west of the Delaware River between New York and Maryland. He had ruling power over the land, which he wanted to name "Sylvania." The King's council added "Penn" to the name. The new colony's name became *Pennsylvania,* which means "Penn's Woods."

In 1682, William Penn, his family, and his followers began a new life in America. Penn and other colonists were Quakers. They believed that all people had the right to religious freedom and to worship as they pleased. In the same year, he signed his first treaty with the Native Americans. In 1684, after the colony was well established, Penn returned to England.

21
31
43
55
66
77

80

92
104
116
126
137
148
154

165
175
186
199
210
217

His Later Years

Penn returned to America in 1699. He granted a new constitution   231
for Pennsylvania, which created a one-house elected assembly.   240
In 1701, however, Penn returned to England because the English   250
government was trying to place the colony under its control.   260
In 1712, while still in England, Penn unfortunately suffered a   270
stroke. This left him paralyzed until his death in 1718. His wife,   282
Hannah, and the colonial secretary, James Logan, handled   290
Penn's affairs in Pennsylvania. His family continued to own   299
the colony of Pennsylvania until the Revolutionary War, when   308
American colonists fought for independence from England. Even   316
after Pennsylvania became a state, it continued to welcome   325
immigrants and Americans from all religious backgrounds.   332
William Penn's belief in religious freedom inspired many people.   341

Lewis and Clark

by Katharine Stevens

New Expedition

In 1803, President Thomas Jefferson sent an expedition to explore
the Louisiana Territory. The United States had bought that land
from the French. Jefferson wanted to know if Americans could
travel west to the Pacific Ocean following the rivers. Jefferson
asked his secretary-aide, Meriwether Lewis, if he would lead the
expedition. Lewis agreed to go, but knew he would need help
for this challenging job. He asked his close friend and former
commanding officer, William Clark, to join him.

Who Were Lewis and Clark?

Lewis and Clark were intelligent and courageous men. Lewis
was born in Virginia in 1774 and grew up near Thomas Jefferson.
As a boy, he explored the woods, learning about plants and
animals. In 1801, Lewis was an Army captain when Thomas
Jefferson offered him a position as his secretary-aide.

Clark was born in Virginia in 1770 and was one of ten children.
His family moved to Kentucky, where they were one of the
earliest settlers. Clark was a lieutenant when Lewis joined the
army in 1794.

 OREGON TERRITORY

SPANISH TERRITORY

The Long Journey

184

Lewis and Clark began their trip on the Missouri River. With a
few boats and forty-five men, they headed for the Pacific Ocean.
Along the way they saw some wildlife that was new to them,
such as coyotes and prairie dogs. Lewis took notes about the
wildlife they saw. Clark drew maps of where they went.

196
208
220
231
241

Their journey was sometimes difficult. The men hunted and
fished but couldn't always find food. Some Native Americans
along the way were friendly, but others were not. Lewis, Clark,
and their men spent the winter with a group of Native Americans
and became friends with a woman named Sacagawea. When
spring came, Sacagawea joined them. She helped them find their
way, speak to Native Americans, and learn which wild foods
were safe to eat.

250
259
270
282
291
301
311
315

After about a year, Lewis and Clark reached the Pacific
Ocean. Then they turned around and traveled all the way home.

325
336

Welcome Home

338

Lewis and Clark's journey took more than two years. Their long
and brave trip opened the American West for settlers. They are
American heroes.

349
360
362

Intervention

A House Divided

by Sara Wayfield

3

6

In 1787, the Northwest Territory joined the United States. American leaders were faced with a big question: Should slavery be allowed in new lands? For the next seventy years, this debate divided the states. Eventually, it started the Civil War.

Slavery did not fit with the freedoms in the Constitution. So American leaders decided that slavery would not be allowed in any future American lands. The debate, however, flared up again.

Fifteen years later, Missouri wanted to join the Union. Slave owners fought hard for slavery to be allowed there. This fight led to the Missouri Compromise.

In 1820, eleven states were free, and eleven allowed slavery. The leaders tried to balance slave and free states. Missouri joined the Union as a slave state, but Maine entered as a free state. A line was drawn across the nation. Owning slaves would be legal only south of the line.

15
25
37
46

57
67
77

87
98
103

113
123
136
147
154

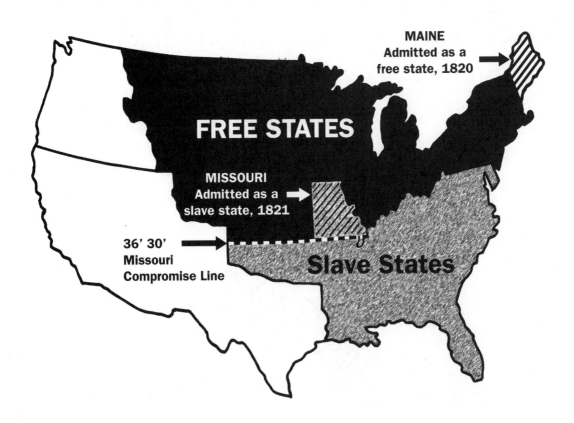

MAINE
Admitted as a free state, 1820

FREE STATES

MISSOURI
Admitted as a slave state, 1821

36' 30'
Missouri Compromise Line

Slave States

In 1850, California wanted to join the Union as a free state. 166
Southerners wanted the right to move west with their slaves. 176
A new compromise was made. California could be free, but the 187
rest of the West would have slavery. 194

Then the Fugitive Slave Act was passed. It said that 204
Northerners must return escaped slaves to their owners. People 213
in the North grew more angry. Most felt slavery was wrong. 224
Now, instead of helping escaped slaves, they must return them 234
to a life of bondage. 239

The Kansas-Nebraska Act was passed in 1854. This law 249
allowed people who lived in these territories to vote about 259
slavery. Groups for and against slavery attacked one another. 268
The territory became known as Bleeding Kansas. 275

In 1857, a slave named Dred Scott sued for his freedom. The 287
Supreme Court decided that only citizens had the right to sue. 298
Dred Scott was returned to slavery. 304

Soon, Abraham Lincoln ran for president. He believed that 313
"A house divided against itself cannot stand." The United States 323
could not be both free and slave-owning. He was elected president 335
in 1860. Southern states knew Lincoln wanted to end slavery. 345
Within months, they left the Union. The Civil War had begun. 356

The Freedom President

by Kristin McDowell

A Land Divided

Abraham Lincoln was elected President of the United States in
1860. He led the United States during the Civil War, the greatest
crisis in American history. Before the war started, there was
a division between the North and the South. The North was
against slavery and welcomed modern ways and change.
Southerners used slave labor to farm the land and did not want
to change their way of life. President Lincoln did not believe
in slavery.

Before Lincoln's inauguration, seven Southern states broke
away from the Union because they thought Lincoln would end
slavery. These seven states formed the Confederate States of
America. In his inaugural address, Lincoln promised that the
Union would use its full power to hold federal possessions in
the Southern states that left the Union.

The War Begins

The Civil War began on April 12, 1861, with the attack of Fort
Sumter, a federal fort in South Carolina. When Lincoln decided
to send supplies to Fort Sumter, the Confederates attacked
the fort. Gunshots and cannons rang out. Smoke filled the air.
Soldiers inside the fort left it two days later. Lincoln quickly
called together an army to fight the Southern soldiers.

Emancipation

During the War, Lincoln took steps to free the slaves. Freeing of the slaves is called *emancipation*. First, he signed a law, the Emancipation Proclamation, which freed the slaves in states at war with the Union. Then, he allowed slaves to fight with Union soldiers against the South.

After the Civil War ended, Lincoln helped push the Thirteenth Amendment through Congress, which abolished slavery throughout the United States.

The South Surrenders

In April of 1865, General Robert E. Lee of the Confederate Army surrendered to General Ulysses S. Grant of the Union Army in Virginia. This ended the war.

A Sad Ending

On April 14, 1865, just five days after the war ended, a Southerner and well-known actor named John Wilkes Booth shot Lincoln. Lincoln was watching a play at the Ford's Theater in Washington. He died the next day. Because of his efforts to free slaves, he'll forever be known as the "Great Emancipator."

A Long Walk Home

by Tom Braveheart

April 21, 1844—

Today was our last day at the camp. By the end of the summer,
I guess Oregon will be home. We have a lot of traveling to do first.

We've camped outside of St. Jo for a week. Hundreds of other
families are here, too. It's the most popular place to rest before
starting on the trails west. Today, Papa told us we leave tomorrow.

I finally get to wear my shoes. My sisters and I got new
shoes before we left Arkansas. Mama wouldn't let us wear them,
though. We're saving them for walking the trail. My bare feet
are so sore and muddy! I'm washing them so they'll be clean
tomorrow for my new shoes.

April 22, 1844—

We didn't leave. Papa spent all morning harnessing oxen to
the wagon and packing up camp. Then Samuel—he's in charge
of our group—said we must wait another day. I could see why.

There were wagons stretched to the horizon. So many families tried to leave at once that the road was too crowded. I saw wagons tipped over and wagons stuck in the mud. Papa grumbled about families from the East. He said they couldn't control their oxen. 173 185 197 207 210

We waited all day. I was happy to have a chance to say good-bye again to my new friends. They are from all over the world. I met a girl from England and a boy from France. I wonder if I'll see them again. 223 236 249 255

April 23, 1844— 258

We finally left this morning. My new shoes hurt my feet even more, so I took them off. Anna, my youngest sister, rode in the wagon. She perched on top of our things. The uneven ground made the wagon sway back and forth. After a while, Anna started crying. The rocking made her sick, so she got down and walked with me. 270 283 294 305 317 320

During the trip, I saw furniture and other belongings dumped along the trail. Papa said people wanted to bring too much with them. "It's like having eyes too big for your stomach," he joked. Will all of our things make it to Oregon? 330 342 354 363

From the Far East to the New West

by Amanda Romero

Did you know that Chinese immigrants lived the frontier life? 21
They don't appear in many photos. Even though history books 31
don't tell much about them, the Chinese played a big role in 43
building the American West. 47

Many Chinese immigrants first came to the United States 56
around 1850. They came for the gold rush in California. Like 67
American pioneers, they wanted to profit from the "Gold 76
Mountain." They were the first large group from Asia to arrive in 88
America. 89

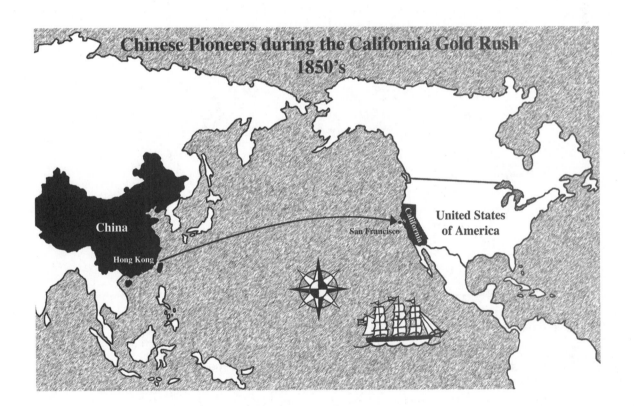

Chinese Pioneers during the California Gold Rush
1850's

Sadly, the Chinese were not treated well. They were not 99
allowed to own property. They also could not become citizens. 109
Their first days on American soil were not easy. Most of the 121
Chinese pioneers were male. They left their families at home. 131
They learned quickly that they were not welcome here. Life must 142
have been lonely. 145

The immigrants formed community groups to support each   153
other. The people in the groups could speak their language and eat   165
familiar foods. This made their hard lives a little easier. Later, these 177
community groups helped the workers fight for their rights. The   187
Chinese fought against unfair laws. Most court decisions were not   197
in their favor, but they kept fighting hard for their freedoms.   208

The Central Pacific Railroad was begun in 1863. The railroad   218
would link the East with the West. Goods could easily travel   229
across the country on trains. Workers were needed to build   239
the tracks, and many Chinese were hired. Their bosses were   249
surprised. The Chinese were model workers. Other railroad   257
men were angry and jealous. The Chinese knew, however, that   267
if they didn't work harder than everyone else, they would lose   278
their jobs. They were right. At one point, Chinese men made up   290
80 percent of the railroad workforce.   296

The Chinese held other jobs in the new West, too. They built   308
bridges and levees. They cleared swamps to make land usable   318
for farming. They were paid less than others who did the same   330
work. Yet they kept working and fighting for their civil rights.   341
Though the Chinese didn't receive much credit for their work,   351
the way they shaped our country will always be a part of our   364
history and theirs.   367

The Town Crier

by Debra Lowery

Rebecca carefully watched as Ben Franklin started his printing press. She enjoyed spending time with him because he always taught her something new. Franklin cranked the machine's largest handle, and the daily newspaper began appearing, one sheet at a time.

14
23
32
40
46

"This is the best printing press," Franklin remarked. "It's so much easier than employing a town crier."

56
63

Rebecca had a puzzled look on her face. "What's a town crier?" she asked.

74
77

Franklin chuckled. "That was before your time, Rebecca, and actually, before my time, too. You see, before 1704, there weren't any regular newspapers in the colonies. Imagine, no newspapers until 26 years ago!"

86
97
106
110

"How did people get their news before that?" Rebecca asked.

120

"That was the town crier's job," Franklin explained. "The town crier marched from street corner to street corner, shouting out the day's important, official messages. Even if it was raining or snowing, the town crier shouted the news. It was a hard job that required a lot of time and energy."

130
140
151
164
171

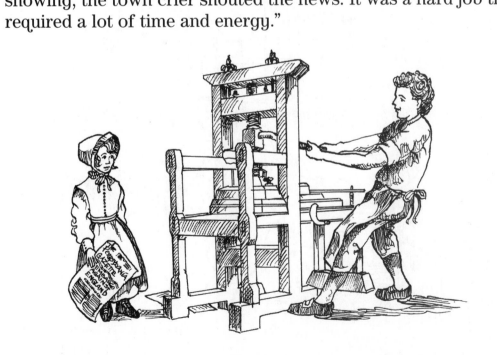

"It sounds like fun to me!" Rebecca cried. "Everyone would be 182
listening to my every word." 187

Both Rebecca and Franklin began laughing. Just then 195
they heard a loud creaking noise from the printing press. The 206
machine suddenly came to a grinding halt. 213

"Oh, no!" Franklin sighed. "The press has stopped working 222
again, today of all days. I need to publicize news of an embargo 235
against England. The embargo forbids all English ships 243
from entering the harbor. But no one will know about it until 255
tomorrow, because it will take the remainder of the day to fix 267
the machine." 269

"I know what we can do!" Rebecca shouted. "Let me be 280
the town crier. Tell me exactly what to say, and I'll shout out 293
the news." 295

Franklin scribbled the message on paper. Rebecca took the 304
sheet from him and ran from the shop. Soon she was standing 316
on a major street corner in town. 323

"Embargo against England!" she shouted proudly. "Come and 331
hear the latest news!" 335

She Was First

by Carol A. Josel

On September 2, 1909, Annie Smith Peck and her two guides
stood on the pointed tip of Mount Huascarán (Hwah scah RAHN)
in Peru. It is one of the highest mountains in the world. Peck
finally had done it!

But Peck was afraid. The wild wind made the cold worse,
and the blowing snow was blinding. Quickly, Peck took pictures
from four directions. The storm grew stronger, and it was
getting dark. Would they make it back to the camp? They slipped
and slid, but foot by foot, they finally reached their tents.

Who was this woman who climbed mountains?

Annie Smith Peck was born in Rhode Island on October 19,
1850. In those times, ladies were taught differently. Like other
girls, she learned to sew and play the piano. But she believed she
could do anything boys could do. She was right.

When the University of Michigan opened to women, she went   160
there and earned an education. She then taught Latin at Purdue   171
University. Later, Peck visited Europe and saw the Matterhorn, a   181
mountain in the Alps, for the first time. She wanted to climb it!   194

Peck needed money to climb, so she wrote speeches and   204
spoke to people who paid to hear her ideas about women's   215
rights. Her speeches helped many people see that everyone must   225
be treated fairly. She believed everyone needed important work   234
to do. Climbing mountains was her important work. Soon Peck   244
had enough money.   247

The Matterhorn was her first mountain, but by 1900, she had   258
climbed twenty! Peck wanted to climb a mountain no one had   269
ever climbed. She picked Huascarán, the greatest mountain in   278
Peru. She tried five times and failed. Frightened guides or bad   289
weather drove her back, but Peck did not give up. In 1909, she   302
and two guides climbed into history.   308

Peck kept climbing. At the age of eighty-two, she climbed   319
Mount Madison in New Hampshire. She is remembered best   328
for mountain climbing. She still is the only woman in history to   340
have been the first to reach the top of one of the world's highest   354
mountains.   355

What Is a Weed?

by Jenette Woollsey

Have you ever wondered why some plants are called weeds?   17
Take dandelions, for instance. They're pretty and don't seem to   27
harm anything. Still, people want to get rid of them. Why?   38

The answer is in how we define weeds. For a gardener, a   50
weed can be a plant that is growing in the wrong place. People   63
who have lawns want green grass, not yellow flowers or the   74
puffballs that dandelion flowers change into. So people get rid   84
of plants that do not fit into the look they want. They call those   98
plants *weeds*.   100

Scientists use a better definition. Some plants kill other plants   110
and harm the land they grow on. They do this by growing fast   123
and taking all the air, good soil, and water in an area. After a   137
while, these plants are the only plants left. Scientists call these   148
plants weeds.   150

Weeds can destroy farmland and gardens. When weeds take   159
over, plants such as corn or wheat cannot grow. In this example,   171
killing weeds is important to human survival.   178

Scientists have worked hard to find ways to kill weeds. The   189
tough part has been to kill them without harming other living   200
things or good plants. Many weed killers can kill insects and   211
animals. They can also harm our air and water.   220

Through many years of study, scientists have found ways to   230
kill weeds while doing little or no harm to other living things.   242
Many years ago, before these ways were found, harsh chemicals   252
were used. The world is still recovering from the harmful effects   263
these chemicals caused. Scientists experiment every day to find   272
safer chemicals and better ways to win the battle against weeds.   283

Some weeds are so pretty that people let them live. That   294
makes them dangerous. One good example is purple loosestrife.   303
You might see pretty purple loosestrife flowers gently blowing   312
in open fields. The problem is that those fields once were full of   325
other colorful wildflowers. The purple loosestrife grew so fast   334
that there wasn't room for other plants. If people had gotten rid   346
of the pretty purple loosestrife right away, the other flowers   356
would still be alive and growing.   362

Getting rid of weeds takes time, but the benefits are clear.   373
The plants and crops grow better and more abundantly. In   383
flower gardens, that means more variety and more beauty.   392

Who Would Eat That?

by Martine Bouret

4
7

Tonio couldn't believe it. Mr. Campos, Tonio's neighbor, was pouring vinegar on a large plant in his backyard. Was Mr. Campos going to eat the plant?

"Mama, Mr. Campos is pouring vinegar on a plant!" said Tonio.

Mama looked out the window. Mr. Campos was pouring a clear liquid from a plastic bottle onto a plant.

"That's just water," laughed Mama.

Mama looked closer at the bottle. It was a little hard to see in the evening darkness, but Tonio was right. Mr. Campos was pouring vinegar on the plant!

"Vinegar can make salad dressing," said Tonio. "I wonder if Mr. Campos is going to eat the plant right in the garden?"

"Of course not!" said Mama. Mr. Campos was very proud of his vegetable garden. He grew wonderful things, like bright red tomatoes, green cucumbers, spicy peppers of all colors, and much more. He shared what he grew with Mama, Tonio, and other neighbors.

The next day, Tonio helped Mr. Campos weed the garden. It 173
was hard work, but he was happy to help Mr. Campos. Weeding 185
was hard on Mr. Campos's knees. 191

As Tonio worked, Mr. Campos looked at the plant he had poured 203
vinegar on. Tonio wondered if Mr. Campos would taste it now. 214

"Tonio, come and look at this," Mr. Campos said suddenly. 224
"This looks really good." 228

Good? Did Mr. Campos want Tonio to taste a leaf of the 240
plant? Tonio walked over to the plant. Its stems and branches 251
had thorns! Its purple flowers were scary looking! *Who would* 261
eat that? Tonio thought with horror. But aloud, Tonio asked, 271
"What kind of plant is it, Mr. Campos?" 279

"It's a Canadian thistle," said Mr. Campos. "It's a weed. I'm 290
trying to get rid of it." 296

"Should I pull it?" said Tonio with a shudder. 305

"No, Tonio," said Mr. Campos. "Pulling it makes seeds drop and 316
more thistle will grow. I read that vinegar mixed with water can 328
kill Canadian thistle. I mixed some and poured it on last night." 340

Tonio looked harder at the weed. The leaves were wilting. 350

"It looks like the vinegar is working," said Mr. Campos. 360
"That's good." 362

"It certainly is," said Tonio. He couldn't wait to tell Mama that 374
vinegar does more than help make a salad dressing. Vinegar 384
kills weeds. 386

A New Light for All

by Duncan Searl

Early in 1878, Thomas Alva Edison made a surprise announcement. He would soon show off his greatest invention ever: the electric light.

There was only one problem. Edison didn't know much about electric light or about how to make a bulb. Of course, he didn't mention that.

Rich men hurried to visit Edison's lab. They set up businesses with Edison and gave the inventor thousands of dollars. "When can we see the light?" they asked. They knew electric lights would change the world. If the bulbs did well, they would become richer.

"Soon," Edison told them. "Soon."

Learning from the Failure of Others

People had tried for half a century to invent electric lights. From their unsuccessful tries, Edison learned he would need three things: a glass bulb without any air in it; a filament, or wire, to put inside the bulb; and electricity to light up the filament.

For the filament, Edison first tried using metal. He literally tried every metal in the world, but nothing worked.

Newspaper reporters came to his lab. "Can we see your electric lights now?" they asked.

"Soon," Edison said, but inside he wasn't so sure. 200

Edison hardly left the lab. Workers made each glass bulb by 211
hand. Putting the filament in could take hours, and the air in the 224
bulb had to be pumped out. Finally, the power was turned on. 236

Dreams Can Come True 240

The bulbs burned for a minute or two, then began to fade. 252
Usually it was because the filament broke, but sometimes 261
the glass bulb cracked. Nothing worked. The rich men and 271
newspapers began to doubt Edison. 276

By accident, Edison learned that carbon filaments worked 284
better than metal. Carbon is what is left behind when you burn 296
something. To find the right carbon, Edison burned string, hair, 306
cork, tar, paper—just about everything. The item that seemed to 317
work the best was burned sewing thread. 324

On December 19th, he tried his 260th light bulb. These bulbs 335
burned longer, some for days on end, so this empowered him to 347
make them better. 350

In late December, Edison hung rows of bright bulbs outside his 361
lab for people to preview. Then he threw the switch. People began 373
to gather around. Never had the world seen a light like this. 385

Edison's first successful light bulb had a filament in the shape 396
of a horseshoe. 399

Ben Franklin's Science Project

by Tamera James

We have all felt the zap of static electricity. It's that little   19
shock we get when we move fast across the carpet and touch a   32
doorknob. Static electricity does not flow like the electricity that   42
runs on wires in a house. But it is still electricity.   53

A long time ago, people felt those small uncomfortable   62
shocks of static electricity. But they did not know much about   73
what caused them. And they did not know how to use electricity   85
to power lights, clocks, and appliances. Therefore scientists   93
wanted to learn more.   97

One of those scientists was Ben Franklin. Franklin was an   107
inventor, a printer, and a writer. He was also one of the founders   120
of the United States.   124

In the 1740s Franklin studied electricity. He did many   133
experiments. He showed how electricity could move from place   142
to place. He found ways to make electric sparks. He also made   154
jars that could hold electric power. But there was one important   165
experiment he still wanted to try.   171

One day in 1752 Franklin flew a kite. It was an undesirable   183
day for kite-flying. Rain fell. Thunder boomed. Lightning flashed.   193

It was the lightning that interested Franklin. Like other   202
scientists, Franklin had a big question. Was lightning electricity?   211
The kite might show him.   216

Franklin's kite had a metal wire on it. He attached a metal   228
key to the bottom of the kite's string. The key was near one of   242
his jars. In the thunderstorm, the kite flew close to a dark cloud.   255
An electric current first transferred from the cloud to the wire   266
in the kite. Next the current traveled fast down the kite string to   279
the key. Then sparks leaped into the jar. Franklin's experiment   289
worked! He now knew that lightning was electricity.   297

Franklin used what he learned to make a new invention. He   308
called it the lightning rod. Years ago, when lightning hit houses,   319
the sparks often caused dangerous fires. The rod made the   329
lightning go straight into the ground before it could start a fire.   341
It made houses and buildings safer. Lightning rods are still   351
used today.   353

Franklin shared his knowledge with other scientists. It would   362
still be a long time before people could flip a switch to turn on a   377
light bulb. But Franklin helped make that day happen sooner.   387

Bees' Feet

by Jeff Reynolds

When we think of bees, we might picture busy hives, honey, and one of the smallest insects buzzing around flowers and picnics on a bright sunny afternoon. We might even think of stingers! But most people don't think about bees' feet. We should. Bees' feet are very important to nature and to us. Why?

If we look carefully at bees in action, we will find out. Bees will most often fly from one flower to another looking for two things—nectar and pollen. Nectar is a food that gives bees energy. It is also what bees use to make honey, wax, and beehives. Pollen is a food that helps bees grow and stay strong. Bees need nectar and pollen to live.

Different kinds of bees get nectar and pollen differently. But the most common characteristic among bees is that they get extra pollen stuck on their feet. If you look closely at films of bees, you might even see the pollen sticking to their feet. Some of that pollen falls off bees' feet when they visit other flowers. That means they take pollen from one flower and drop it into another.

16
26
37
48
59

71
82
94
107
119
126

136
146
159
171
183
194
196

Pollen falling off bees' feet may seem like an accident, but it   208
is one of the most important steps in helping new flowers grow.   220
For plants, pollen is the key to life. Pollen that has moved from   233
one flower to another is necessary in making new plants. If this   245
did not happen, plants would die out. If plants died out, people   257
would die out too. We need plants to provide food, clean air, and   270
clean water.   272

Flowering plants and bees have a symbiotic relationship.   280
Each one gets something important from the other. Bees live on   291
pollen and the sweetest nectar from plants. Plants depend on   301
bees to make new plants grow. This relationship keeps humans   311
alive as well. So much depends on the tiniest feet of little bees!   324
So next time you see a bee, think twice before swatting it.   336

Weeds!

by Olivia Miyar

Brendan couldn't believe it. Grandma's yard was covered
with weeds! The night before, when Mom had dropped him
off at Grandma's house, it had been one of the darkest nights
ever. He hadn't seen the weeds then. But now, in the early
morning sunlight, they couldn't be missed. The weeds were
tall and brightly colored, but they were still weeds. Where was
Grandma's lawn?

Brendan thought it was strange that Mom hadn't mentioned
the weeds to him. But Mom did mention a couple of other things
last night. She said to help Grandma around the house and to
keep thinking about the school science fair project he had to do
next month.

While Grandma was in the kitchen making breakfast,
Brendan had an idea. He could help Grandma by pulling some
of the weeds. As he started to work, Brendan had another idea.
Maybe he could do a science project about weeds and how they
were the most awful things for lawns.

A few minutes later, Grandma glanced out the kitchen   175
window and saw Brendan pulling up her most precious plants.   185
Grandma walked to the back door. "Brendan, you don't have to   196
pick those," she said. "They're not weeds. They're prairie plants."   206

Brendan stopped working. "Prairie plants?" he said.   213

"Yes, prairie plants grow the deepest in the ground and   223
highest into the air of all grass," Grandma said. "They are one   235
of the safest things for the earth and the atmosphere."   245

"Oh," said Brendan with a frown. "I thought they were weeds.   256
I wanted to help you."   261

"I know," said Grandma with a smile. "Don't feel bad. You   272
can help me plant my favorite plants after we eat breakfast.   283
While we work, I'll tell you how the prairie plants also help keep   296
water clean, stop flooding, and give birds and animals good   306
places to live."   309

Brendan felt better. He was going to help Grandma work   319
in her prairie—and he had a tremendous idea for his science   331
project. It would be about prairie plants and why they are good   343
for the earth and the air.   349

Intervention

Rock or Mineral?

by Hector Cedeño

Rocks can be found everywhere. There are tiny pebbles on beaches and big stones in fields. Rocky mountains stand tall over cities. If you dig deep under your lawn, you'll find rock. If you walk on the bottom of the ocean, you'll walk on rock.

Can you define what a rock is? Here's the simplest way: A rock is the combination of one or more minerals. That's easy—if you know what a mineral is.

A mineral is nonliving, solid, natural matter. *Nonliving* means a mineral is not a plant, animal, or other living thing. Gold is a mineral. A true mineral was never a living thing. Therefore a piece of wood is not a mineral. It was once part of a living thing, a tree.

We say that a mineral is *natural.* That means that a mineral cannot be made by people. Iron is found in rock all over the earth. Steel is something people must make from iron. We can conclude, then, that iron is a mineral and steel is not. Here's another thing to remember: minerals are not rocks; minerals mix together to form rocks.

144
157
168
180
190
194

There are many kinds of minerals. Some are hard. Some are 205
soft. Some look shiny. Some look dull. Minerals come in all sizes, 217
even the same kind of mineral. For example, gold can be found 229
as tiny particles or in larger pieces. 236

The same mineral might look a little different at times. But 247
check it out with a microscope. Then the tiniest bit of gold 259
always looks the same. 263

All living things need to take in certain minerals. You need 274
minerals for healthy bones, teeth, blood, and muscles. These 283
minerals can be found in some rocks. But that doesn't mean you 295
will be cooking rocks and putting them on your dinner table! 306
We get these minerals through regular food. Humans also use 316
minerals to make jewelry, chalk, cement, and much more. By 326
digging into the earth we can find silver, iron, and gold. But not 339
all minerals we use come from rock. For example, we can take 351
the mineral salt from the sea. 357

People of all ages collect rocks. They can also name the 368
minerals in a rock. Want a good science project? Display rocks 379
and minerals. 381

Leading the Way

by Pam Conrad

3
6

Meet Shannon Lucid. She is a mother, a scientist, and an astronaut. She also holds a world record. Her record is for the longest time a woman has spent in space—more than six months.

In late March 1996, Lucid blasted off from Earth in the space shuttle *Atlantis*. She arrived at the space station *Mir* on March 23. Lucid lived on *Mir* for the next 188 days.

Lucid ate, slept, exercised, and worked on *Mir*. She fixed her meals in the station's kitchen. Lucid mixed dried foods such as meat, rice, and pudding with water. If she let go of her spoon, it floated like a leaf suspended in water. She was comfortable either right side up or upside down.

Lucid says that living in space is fun. It can also cause problems. For example, everyone who goes into space loses muscle. In addition, living in space can cause bones to weaken. This is because the lack of gravity makes it easier for bones and muscles to support weight. They don't have to work as hard, so they lose strength. Exercise helps keep people's bones and muscles strong. She trained like an athlete to stay in shape. She rode an exercise bike and ran on a treadmill. She exercised a total of almost four hundred hours.

Lucid was asked to conduct experiments. She found out how a candle can burn in space. She studied how space affects the way baby birds grow inside eggs. Her experiments will help other scientists learn more about life in space.

Finally it was time for Lucid to return. A crew boarded *Atlantis*, traveled into space, and docked with *Mir*. The crew transferred food, supplies, and air to the space station. Crew member John Blaha was going to stay. Then Lucid and the rest of the crew headed for home. On September 26, 1996, the *Atlantis* crew and Lucid arrived safely at Cape Canaveral.

After Lucid returned, other scientists were eager to talk with her. They wanted to do medical tests. Scientists knew the information they gathered could help them understand the effects of living in space for long periods of time. This information could also make space travel easier in the future.

Congratulations, Shannon Lucid. And thank you for leading the way!

139
148
159
172
183
193
205
217
223

233
245
255
263

274
284
294
305
317
326

335
345
353
365
375

383
385

You Can Use the Scientific Method

by Alice Nichols

Can you be a scientist? Scientists use something called the scientific method to figure things out. You can use it, too, in a science project.

Step 1: *Describe the purpose of your project.* For example, have you heard that putting eggshells in the ground helps plants grow taller? Is this true? Answering that question can be the purpose of your science project.

Step 2: *Create a hypothesis.* When you use the scientific method, you need to have a hypothesis. A hypothesis is something that is suggested as being true. You need to research some facts to assist in helping you with a hypothesis. For example, here's a fact about eggshells: They are made of calcium, a mineral. And here's a fact about calcium: It can help some things grow.

With those facts, you might come up with this hypothesis:

1. Eggshells have calcium.

2. Calcium helps things grow.

3. So eggshells help plants grow.

Step 3: *Test your hypothesis.* Think of how you will prove your hypothesis is true. Scientists set up an experiment so one thing is different. For example, you could have ten plants in your basement. All ten would be exactly the same kind of plant. And they would be exactly the same size.

Each plant would be growing in a separate flowerpot. Each would be treated exactly the same, except for one thing. In five of the flowerpots, you would put ground eggshells. In the other five, you would not.

Then you would watch your plants grow. When they are grown, you will measure each plant. Did the five that grew with eggshells grow more than, less than, or the same amount as the other five plants? Your experiment will tell you if eggshells—the one thing that was different—helped the plants.

Step 4: *Perform the experiment.* As you do, take notes. Work to make certain only one thing is really different between each group of plants: eggshells.

Step 5: *Check your hypothesis.* After your experiment is over, ask if your hypothesis was true. Do eggshells help plants grow? Or were your results unclear? Do you need to retry the experiment?

Now describe your experiment in a written report.

Bonus Step Bring the plants to the school science fair. Draw a big chart and make copies of your report. Everyone will be impressed. And you will be a scientist!

Millions of Microbes

by Andrew Kodali

You can't see them, but they are everywhere. They are in the food you eat, the water you drink, and the air you breathe. They are in your bed, on your pillow, and on your sheets. What are they? They are microbes. They are tiny living things that are too small for you to see with your eyes alone.

For most of human history, no one knew about these tiny creatures. That changed when Antoni van Leeuwenhoek looked through his microscope in 1676. In a drop of water, he saw very small things swimming around. As years passed, he kept a record of the creatures he put under his microscope. He even found them in food that had been stuck between his teeth!

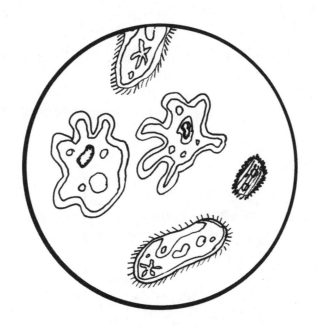

To Leeuwenhoek, these tiny things looked like animals. He even called them *animalcules*. They look for food, protect their lives, and reproduce.

Billions and billions of microbes live this way in and out of your body. If that sounds like bad news, it isn't. Most microbes are good for you. In fact, you need them to live. Microbes help you digest food. They help your heart beat. They help your body in many ways.

139
149
152

164
176
189
201
204

Most of the microbes found in your body are called bacteria.   215
Sometimes bacteria are called germs. Some bacteria can make   224
you sick. But, most bacteria do not cause illness.   233

Another kind of microbe is fungus. This microbe can be   243
very helpful. For example, yeast is a fungus that helps bread   254
to rise. And fungi are used to make the antibiotics we take   266
when we get sick. However, some fungi can be harmful. The   277
rash called athlete's foot is a fungus. And fungus is what makes   289
bread moldy.   291

Have you ever seen water in a swimming pool turn green?   302
Algae, another kind of microbe, do that. Algae are part of a   314
big group of microbes called protists. Like plants, algae can   324
make oxygen. Since most living things need oxygen, algae   333
are important.   335

Should you worry about the harmful microbes? Doing things   344
to take care of yourself—eating well, washing your hands, and   355
getting plenty of sleep—keeps the bad microbes away. The   365
important thing to remember is that without microbes to help   375
you, there would be no you!   381

The First Trains of the West

by Alicia Rodriguez

Today we travel in cars, and we ride in buses and trains. Airplanes can take us to far away places very quickly. But travel was not as easy for the pioneers. They lived before cars and airplanes. The pioneers traveled many, many miles to their new homes in the West. Pioneers rode in covered wagons. They were large enough to carry everything a family would need to make a new start in their new home. The wagons were made of wood and covered with heavy cloth. Sometimes teams of horses pulled the wagons. Other times, oxen led the way.

A wagon train was a group of covered wagons that moved together. The wagon trains were long. There could be forty wagons in the train. A lot of people could travel together. This allowed the people to help each other. If one wagon broke, the wagons stopped. Everyone helped fix the broken wagon.

Because the West had no real roads, the wagon trains moved over rough trails. They crossed streams and rivers. Some rivers were deep. The wagons had to float across. Each day of the trip was hard.

The covered wagons were heavy. Each wagon carried pots, pans, and other things for the kitchen. They carried furniture and tools. They carried clothes, and they even carried a few books. Food was packed too. The wagons carried bacon, flour, rice, and beans. Dried fruit was a special treat. The pioneers cooked meals over fires and ate their food on tin dishes. Even cows and chickens went with the trains. The cows followed the wagons. The chickens were in cages. 206 216 227 237 248 260 271 277

Sometimes people brought too much on their trip. They would unload the extra things and leave them on the side of the road or try to sell them to others. Traveling as light as possible was important because the trip was very long. 287 300 313 320

The people got their water from barrels. The barrels were packed on a water wagon. The water wagons were very important. Trips were often hot and dusty, so the pioneers and their families got very thirsty. 330 340 351 356

At night, the wagons made a big circle. Most people slept in the wagons. Someone always stayed awake to watch for wild animals. When the sun rose, the wagon train moved on again. Another day would bring the pioneers closer to their new home. 368 378 389 400

Wagon Ho!

by Robin Goldman

The pink sun was rising in the morning sky. Liz rubbed   16
her sleepy eyes. She smelled the bacon cooking and knew it   27
was time to get up. Today would be better than yesterday.   38
Yesterday the rain and mud had made travel hard. The wagons   49
had traveled only one mile. When the wagon train stopped, Liz   60
had many chores to do. She milked the cows and fetched water   72
from the stream. She helped her father gather wood for the fire.   84
Yesterday she had to do all those chores in the chilly rain.   96

Today, however, the sun was shining. The wagon train could   106
move seven miles or more, and Liz was ready. She wanted to   118
reach the new land her parents talked about. She thought about   129
the green grass where the animals could graze. And she dreamed   140
about her new home.   144

"Wagon Ho!" shouted the captain of the wagon train. The   154
wagons moved forward. *Bump, bump, bump.* They were heavy   163
from the loads they were carrying. Liz's wagon had almost   173
everything her family needed for a new start. Liz rode in the   185
wagon for a while. Then she got tired of the bumps. She decided   198
to walk. She followed the cows that were tied to the wagons.   210
I wonder if they're as tired as I am, she thought.   221

The sun was high in the sky when the wagon train slowed   233
to a stop. Lunch was made and eaten quickly. Everyone on the   245
train was ready for a rest. Liz lay down under a pine tree. Two   259
hours seemed like minutes. She awoke to the usual, "Wagon Ho!"   270

On and on the wagon train rolled. Liz was glad when late   282
afternoon shadows fell across the wagon train. The wagons   291
pulled into a circle. Liz helped her mother with dinner while the 303
others took care of the animals. Soon, darkness fell. Everyone   313
gathered around the campfire. Liz liked to sing the campfire   323
songs. And she loved that drowsy feeling the warm fire brought.   334
Liz fell asleep and dreamed again of a land that was beautiful   346
and green.   348

Liz awoke to the sound of the captain's morning call. Liz was   360
ready. She knew this "Wagon Ho!" might just be the one to take   373
her home.   375

Building a River

by Mathew Watson

Sitting in the attic, Eliza opened an old box. In it, she found a
stack of postcards wrapped in twine. Each had a different drawing
of what looked like a river. On some cards, it ran among fields and
valleys; on others, it flowed through busy towns. The backs of each
card were blank, except one. That card had a spidery signature:
DeWitt Clinton. Eliza grabbed the stack and ran downstairs.

She landed on the couch beside her dad. "What are these?"

He squinted and grinned. "They're postcards of the Erie
Canal. They belonged to my great-, great-, great-, great-
grandfather, Daniel Stover."

"So, who was DeWitt Clinton?"

"Clinton was governor of New York. It was his idea to build the
Erie Canal. Many people, including Thomas Jefferson, thought it
was a terrible idea. Clinton knew that a waterway between Lake
Erie and the Hudson River in New York would create big changes.
It opened trade between the East and the Midwest."

"What about Daniel?"

"He helped build the canal," answered Dad. "It was 363 miles 182
long, forty feet wide, and four feet deep," he added. "Would you 194
believe the canal was dug by hand?" 201

Eliza looked closely at the card. "Are animals pulling that 211
boat?" she asked, surprised. 215

"Yes. Boats were pulled by teams of mules or oxen. Young 226
boys, called hoggees, led the animals along a path beside the 237
canal. A few of Daniel's brothers and sons were hoggees. Some 248
were as young as eight." 253

"They didn't go to school?" asked Eliza. "That might have 263
been fun for a while, but I wouldn't want to work like that my 277
whole life." 279

Dad nodded. "It was hard work, but Daniel was proud of it. 291
Everyone celebrated the day the canal opened in 1825. Cannons 301
along the canal blasted one after another, all the way from 312
Buffalo to New York City. Governor Clinton poured water from 322
Lake Erie into New York Harbor. It was called 'the wedding of 334
the waters.'" 336

"Did Clinton sign this card for Daniel?" asked Eliza. 345

Dad smiled. "Yes. Clinton congratulated Daniel for his hard 354
work. Daniel stood for all the workers who made such an 365
incredible dream real." 368

"This is amazing," Eliza said, as she stood up. "Do you think 380
I can find other family treasures upstairs?" 387

A Bridge to the Future

by Janet Edges

|---|---|
| | 5 |
| | 8 |

On May 24, 1883, the Brooklyn Bridge opened. It stretched　18
across the East River from Brooklyn to the island of Manhattan.　29
At the time, it was the longest suspension bridge on Earth.　40
The bridge's towers were the tallest structures in America. The　50
Brooklyn Bridge was a marvel of design and engineering.　59

After the Civil War, America prospered. Railroad building　67
created many jobs. The new steel industry thrived. Canals and　77
railroads carried people and goods around the nation. The　86
American economy boomed.　89

John Augustus Roebling came to America from Germany　97
for a better life. He was an engineer, and he used his skills to　111
develop his career. During the 1840s and 1850s, he built canals　122
and bridges throughout the eastern half of the United States.　132

Roebling's bridges were special because he used steel ropes.　141
Rope made from metal was much stronger than fiber rope.　151
Roebling understood that steel rope was the key to building　161
bigger bridges. This idea helped him build a bridge across the　172
Ohio River in Cincinnati. It was the longest suspension bridge　182
in the world. Roebling's reputation was set.　189

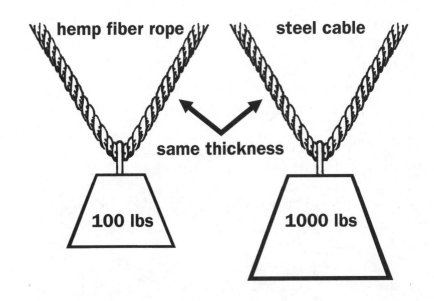

In the 1860s, New Yorkers planned to build a bridge between 200
Manhattan and Brooklyn. Who could take on such a difficult 210
project? Roebling was the answer. He agreed to the challenge. 220

Before work began, though, tragedy struck. In 1869, 228
Roebling's foot was crushed by a ferry. He died a few weeks 240
later. Roebling's son, Washington, took over. He was equally 249
talented but just as unlucky. Poor working conditions made 258
Washington ill. Three years into the project, he was too sick to 270
leave his bed. He used a telescope to observe the construction. 281

Washington's wife, Emily, took over. At first, she ran 290
messages from her husband to the job site. As the years passed, 302
though, Emily handled more. She even went to school to learn 313
about engineering. By the time the bridge was done, Emily was 324
mostly in charge of the project. 330

The Brooklyn Bridge took fourteen years to build. On opening 340
day, Emily Roebling was the first person to cross it. More than 352
one hundred fifty thousand people followed her. Many workers 361
had been European immigrants. The bridge's gothic architecture 369
reminded them of old churches in Europe. At the same time, the 381
Brooklyn Bridge was built with modern methods. It linked two 391
pieces of land, but it was a bridge to America's future, too. 403

Letters from the Golden West

by Alexis Gooding

5

8

11

13

24

36

48

60

72

85

95

105

117

129

143

155

161

September 19, 1849

Dear Charlie,

I'm in California. *Hot* and *dusty* are the only words to describe my trip. Every person on the trail was going West with the same goal—to strike it rich. People helped one another, but it was strange. Everyone hurried to get here and stake a claim. No one could help trying to move faster than the man beside him. So many people are headed to this land. No one knows how much gold there is or how long it will last.

I was wiser in my preparations than many. Thank your mama for her good advice. Many men ran out of water early. My supply lasted until the final two days. It could have lasted the whole way. But in Nevada, I traded a jug for five pounds of bacon—a good trade. In the desert, a man paid twenty-seven dollars for a glass of water!

I'm glad I grew up on a farm. Plenty of men on the trail had 176
never owned a horse or fixed a wagon wheel. City life can't 188
teach a person everything! I'm tired to the bone, so I'm turning 200
in now. I'll write again in a few weeks. Give my love to everyone. 214

Your uncle, 216

Louis Montaine 218

October 14, 1849 221

Dear Charlie, 223

I hope the family is doing well. California is a strange place. 235
It's odd without government or laws. It's freeing in a way, but the 248
attitude is "every man for himself." I prefer a few rules to keep 261
folks in order. 264

I found gold my first day panning. That was a feeling I won't 277
forget! I'm making enough money to survive, but I can't save a 289
penny. Everything is scarce, so prices are high. With each day 300
that passes, though, a new business comes to the area. I wonder 312
if the business folks are wiser than the miners with their picks 324
and shovels. 326

Most nights I'm too tired to dream. When I do, I see piles of 340
shiny gold in the sun. I see your mama standing in the yard of 354
a pretty white house. I see you studying for school. And I see 367
myself with a handsome farm and a team of first-class racing 379
horses. You keep dreaming, Charlie. I'll do the same. 388

Your loving uncle, 391

Louis Montaine 393

The World Comes to Chicago

by Carla Leal

In May 1893, the Chicago World's Fair opened. It was   18
very different from the fairs of today. This fair marked the   29
anniversary of Christopher Columbus's arrival in America.   36
For this reason, it was also known as the World's Columbian   47
Exposition. An exposition is a display. All the latest inventions   57
from around the globe were on display.   64

Fairs do not last forever, but that didn't stop the planners   75
from thinking big. More than two hundred buildings were built   85
just for the fair. Parts of them were made from cheap materials.   97
Though they looked wonderful, the buildings were not meant to   107
stand the test of time. Only one still stands today.   117

One set of buildings was made in a classical style. They   128
looked like Greek and Roman buildings, with pillars, domes, and   138
arches. Because every building was painted white, they were   147
called the White City. This modeled what a perfect city might   158
look like.   160

The Chicago World's Fair was a place to show off the latest   172
advances in technology. Electricity was still new to America.   181
An entire building held electrical displays. There, one could see   191
the first neon lights and an early form of the fluorescent light.   203
President Grover Cleveland flipped a switch in the White House,   213
hundreds of miles from the fair. Like magic, the White City lit up. 226
People were excited by the promise of electricity.   234

The Ferris wheel was another first at the Chicago World's   244
Fair. It was 250 feet tall and had thirty-six cars. The wheel was   258
powered by two steam engines. It took twenty minutes to make   269
one full turn. George Ferris designed the wheel to be the main   281
attraction at the fair.   285

People also saw Thomas Edison's kinetograph. It was an early   295
type of moving picture. There were all sorts of odd, amazing   306
things to be seen. Where else could you find a map of the   319
United States made of pickles or a book from the *Mayflower*?   330
What about a block of cheese that weighed twenty-two   340
thousand pounds?   342

The fair closed in October 1893. It cost more than thirty   353
million dollars and was open for six months. During that time,   364
more than twenty-seven million people visited. Some stayed only   374
a day or two. Others stayed for a week. Everyone knew they   386
were part of something special—something that would go down   396
in history.   398

Remember the *Maine!*

by Kali Manuel

In February 1898, the USS *Maine* floated in the harbor
outside Havana, Cuba. Cuba was a Spanish colony, but Cubans
had started to rebel. They wanted to rule their own country.
The *Maine*, an American battleship, waited in the harbor for a
month. Its job was to protect American fruit farms. The ship's
officers hoped for a peaceful end to the uprising.

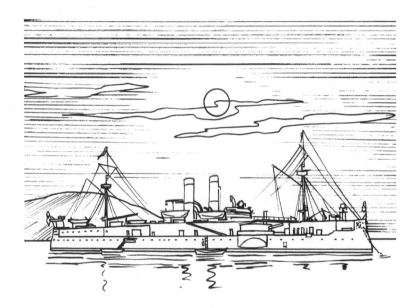

Instead, an explosion shattered the quiet February night.
The blast split the *Maine* in half. It caught fire and was sinking
fast. Other ships rushed to help, but hundreds of sailors
died that night. Even today, no one knows for sure why the
Maine exploded.

In the United States, though, most people blamed the Spanish.
For months, newspapers had been reporting Spanish injustice
toward the Cubans. Support for a war against Spain grew.
Remember the Maine! became a popular saying. Eventually
President McKinley declared war.

The Spanish-American War began thousands of miles
from Cuba in another Spanish colony in the middle of the
Pacific Ocean. It was the Philippines. On May 1, the American
navy attacked without warning. The Spanish navy was
quickly defeated.

Then fighting began in Cuba. After a few months of difficult 204
fighting, the war reached a standstill. American and Spanish 213
troops were deadlocked. Something had to be done. Future 222
president Teddy Roosevelt brought a ragtag group of fighters 231
called the Rough Riders to Cuba. They included cowboys and 241
Native Americans from the West, policemen from big cities in the 252
East, and athletes Roosevelt knew in college. They were nearly 262
as diverse as America itself. 267

The Rough Riders waited with American troops at the bottom 277
of San Juan Hill. The officers took a long time deciding what to 290
do next. Roosevelt was impatient; he led his men into action. 301
The Rough Riders stormed the hill. The Battle of San Juan Hill 313
had begun. 315

Charging beside the Rough Riders was the 10th Cavalry. 324
Better known as the Buffalo Soldiers, this unit of African 334
American fighters cleared the way for other troops. The battle 344
cost many people their lives, but the Americans won. Roosevelt 354
was hailed as a hero. 359

The Spanish-American War lasted only a few months, but 369
America would never be the same. The United States took over 380
many of Spain's colonies. The Philippines, Guam, and Puerto 389
Rico were now American land. America had great influence in 399
Cuba, too. America was becoming a superpower. 406

A City of Opportunity

by Nate Williams

Willie and his cousin, Lloyd, walked through the
neighborhood. Willie wasn't used to the city's lights. They hung
along both sides of the street and shone from every storefront.
Though it was night, Willie could see as clear as day. There was
so much noise! Willie could not imagine getting used to it.

Lloyd's dad, Walt, brought his family north so he could work
in an auto factory. Soon after they settled, he wrote a letter to
his brother Sam, Willie's dad. He said life was great in Detroit.
There was plenty of work and all sorts of modern entertainment.
And there were no Jim Crow laws. African Americans were
not forced to be separate from white people. They did not have
different restaurant tables, train cars, and doorways.

Willie's family had always lived in Alabama. His dad had
enjoyed working the land. Of course, it wasn't his land. Sam
dreamed of buying his own farm, but the white land owners
didn't sell to African Americans.

Moving north was a big decision, but Sam was tired of the   185
Jim Crow laws. A week after Walt's letter arrived, Sam watched   196
Willie enter Gus's General Store through the door marked for   206
African Americans. Sam knew that Willie didn't think about why   216
he couldn't use the front door. Sam made his decision.   226

Now Sam worked at the same factory his brother did. The   237
family lived in a small apartment, but it was big enough for the   250
three of them. Willie was shocked to find out that the landlord   262
was an African American man! Willie soon realized that African   272
Americans owned many things in his neighborhood. An African   281
American man even owned the theater where the two families   291
were headed that night.   295

The idea of moving pictures seemed so strange to Willie. He   306
had seen plenty of photographs, but he couldn't understand how   316
someone had gotten them to move. The families stopped at the   327
box office window. Sam insisted on buying tickets for everyone.   337
His brother protested, but Sam stood firm. He told Walt he   348
owed him more than theater tickets. Then Sam stood back and   359
watched everyone enter the theater through the front door.   368

The Roaring Twenties

by Rachel Rivera

The Great War—now known as World War I—had finally ended. Fifteen million people died and Europe was in ruins. American soldiers came home in 1918. They were saddened by the violence they'd seen. It was time for a new era.

The 1920s are often called the Roaring Twenties. A carefree America emerged from the dark days of WWI. The soldiers had money to spend from their military pay. For the first time, women entered the workforce in large numbers. A new African American middle class grew in the big cities. The American economy grew stronger.

The decade began with a breakthrough for women's rights. The Nineteenth Amendment became law in 1920, giving women the right to vote. A decade full of changes for women had begun! During WWI, while American men fought in Europe, women did many of the men's jobs. Most women enjoyed their new roles and freedoms. Women couldn't give that up once the men returned.

17
27
37
48

58
68
80
90
100
103

112
121
134
144
156
166

Fashions changed for women, too. Corsets, which had bound women's bodies for decades, weren't worn any longer. Flapper style—short hair, loose dresses, and lots of dancing—became popular. Women began sharing their ideas and opinions in public.

175
184
194
204

In most big cities, an African American middle class 213
developed. In New York, an area called Harlem became the 223
center of African American culture. Art, literature, politics, and 232
music, including jazz, flourished there. The time became known 241
as the Harlem Renaissance. 245

Jazz began as an African American form of music. It swept 256
the nation during the Twenties. Its jumping rhythms and upbeat 266
melodies fit the nation's mood. Everyone wanted to have a good 277
time. Sometimes the 1920s are even called the Jazz Age. Jazz 288
caused new respect for African American culture. 295

The strong economy meant that people had plenty of money 305
to spend. People began going to the movies. They spent money 316
on many new products. The most important was the automobile. 326
Millions of people bought their first cars during the Twenties. 336
This meant that roads needed to be built, which meant even 347
more jobs. The nation was zipping along. 354

Of course, nothing lasts forever. In October 1929, the stock 364
market crashed. Many people lost the money they had invested 374
as a result of the crash. It was a signal of bad days to come. 389
Economies all over the world began to crumble. The Roaring 399
Twenties were over. The Great Depression was about to begin. 409

Tessa Takes to the Air

by Frances Gilles

Tessa Nichol tightly gripped her father's hand as they walked across the airfield. Her heart felt like a tiny animal fighting to get out of a trap. She was scared, but she was excited, too!

Mr. Nichol quickly squeezed Tessa's hand and strode ahead to shake hands with the pilot. Tessa was proud of her handsome papa. Mr. Nichol had a way with people. He always knew the most interesting folks. He met Mr. Kresman at a party, and the two men became fast friends. Today they were co-owners of the shiny plane that sat on the runway.

"Have you met my daughter, Tessa?" Mr. Nichol asked. He put one arm around Tessa's shoulder and smiled.

"Pleased to meet you," said Tessa.

"So this is the brave little lady who's flying with us today," said Mr. Kresman. "I have something for you," he said, pulling out a leather aviator jacket just her size.

The two men walked around the plane, thumping on different parts. Tessa stared at the propellers and the outstretched wings. Two seagulls flew overhead, calling loudly. Tessa grinned. Soon she'd be flying, too.

A few minutes later, Tessa's entire body vibrated as the   205
plane's engine roared to life. The plane began moving, and Tessa   216
held her breath. The trees beside the runway became a blur as   228
the plane gathered speed. Suddenly they were in the air. For a   240
moment, Tessa's stomach did flips. Then she looked around and   250
completely forgot about her stomach. What a sight!   258

"What do you think?" yelled Mr. Nichol.   265

"It's amazing!" Tessa shouted back. She got a glimpse of the   276
city. The buildings had always seemed so huge. Right now, they   287
looked like toys that Tessa could scoop up and put in her pocket.   300

"Just twenty years ago, people laughed at the Wright Brothers   310
and their 'flying machine,'" said Tessa's papa. "They didn't   319
believe, Tessa. That's what this country is all about, believing in   330
yourself and believing in the future."   336

As they circled Lady Liberty standing proudly in New York   346
Harbor, Tessa believed. She thought her heart might burst with   356
happiness. "One day, I'm going to fly this plane myself," she   367
said above the rumble of the engine. Her father only nodded.   378
He knew she would do exactly that.   385

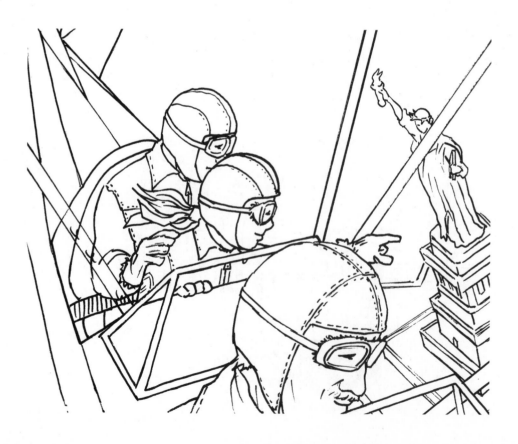

Intervention

The Dollar Bill

by Anchal Singh

What is money made of? Though it looks and feels like paper, it isn't paper. Money is actually made from cloth. The cloth is made up of two different fibers, cotton and linen. There are also red and blue silk strands running through this cloth. These strands run through the entire bill.

Money does not fall apart when it gets wet. That's because it's cloth, not paper! A special ink is also used on money. This ink does not smear or smudge when a bill gets wet. The ink is made from a secret recipe so people can't duplicate it.

In the middle of a dollar bill, there is a picture of one of our country's former leaders. Most of these pictures are of former presidents. Can you name which president is on the one dollar bill? How about the five dollar bill? Washington is on the one dollar bill, and Lincoln is on the five dollar bill. Having your likeness, or face, imprinted on American money is an important honor.

The U.S. Treasury Seal is also on the front of a dollar bill. This seal is bright green. On the top of the seal is a scale. Some people say the scale stands for a balanced budget. A *budget* shows "how much money you plan to earn and spend." Other people think the scale stands for justice. Thirteen stars are in the center of the seal. The stars stand for the first thirteen colonies.

18
30
41
52
58

70
83
97
106

121
131
143
156
169
177

190
205
216
227
239
251

Two circles on the back of the bill show two sides of the   264
Great Seal of the United States. In the left circle, there is a   277
pyramid. It stands for the country's strength. In the right circle,   288
there is the Seal of the President of the United States. An eagle   301
is on this seal. No one knows for sure what the eagle means.   314
Perhaps the eagle stands for strength. Maybe it stands for   324
freedom. What do you think?   329

There are thirteen stars above the eagle. The stars also   339
represent the first thirteen colonies. The eagle is holding an   349
olive branch and arrows. The olive branch and arrows stand for   360
peace and war. In between the two sides of the Great Seal of the   374
United States is the motto, "In God We Trust."   383

The dollar bill is full of history. It tells the story of when our   397
land was new. Look at a dollar bill. What else do you see?   410

We Can Bank On It

by Pamela Golden

Where should people save money? In a piggy bank? In an old sock? No! The best place is in a savings account at a bank. Not only will the bank keep money safe, but it will also pay people for saving their money. A piggy bank can't do that! How does a bank pay people for having an account? The answer is a bank's main business: lending money.

A bank lends money to people and businesses. People borrow money to buy houses, cars, and boats. They borrow money to help pay for college. Businesses borrow money to build new factories or stores, to get new equipment, and so on. There are many reasons for individuals and businesses to borrow money from a bank. A good, strong bank can help many businesses grow strong.

When people and businesses borrow money, they pay it back to the bank a little at a time. They also pay interest. Interest is the cost people and businesses pay for borrowing money from a bank. Interest is also how the bank makes money from these loans.

A bank uses interest from loans for several things. It uses 191
some of it to pay employees and for other banking costs. A 203
bank also pays some of that interest to people who have savings 215
accounts. Why? It's simple. The money the bank lends comes 225
from the people who have savings accounts. Since it uses their 236
money for loans, the bank should pay them. The amount the 247
bank pays is also called interest. 253

So what happens when someone wants to withdraw, or take 263
out, money from his or her savings account? Since the bank 274
uses it for loans, will it still be there? Yes. A bank has to keep a 290
reserve of cash on hand. This "extra," or reserve, allows a bank 302
to give people their money whenever they want it. 311

In the meantime, money stored in a bank is very safe. A bank 324
has a giant vault. Every night its doors are locked and cash is 337
stored securely inside. Money in a bank is safe in other ways, 349
too. Laws make sure a bank will return any money people might 361
save with it. A savings account is a very good place to keep 374
money. That's something we can all bank on! 382

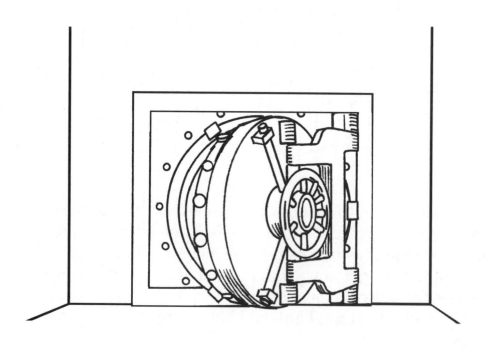

From Village to City

by Jonathan Stewart

Some villages grow into large cities because of their location. People need ways to make a living, so cities grow in places that make earning money easier. Chicago's location on the shores of Lake Michigan is an example.

17
30
40
45

More than five thousand years ago, Native Americans lived near the lake. They canoed on the lake and rivers around it. One of those rivers, the Checagou, meaning "great or powerful," flowed into the lake. Another river, the Des Plaines, was just a few miles away. The two rivers did not connect, so people carried canoes from one to the other. From the Des Plaines River, travelers could reach the Mississippi River.

54
66
76
87
99
110
117

The rivers and lake brought different groups of Native Americans together from many places to trade with each other. They traded pottery, animal furs, arrowheads, and food. Much of the travel and trade took place where the Checagou River met the lake.

126
136
145
157
159

Then Europeans came to America. Many wanted to become 168
wealthy. Some knew this location would be great for trade. In 179
1673, a French explorer wanted to dig a canal to link the two 192
rivers to make trading easier. But no canal was built at that time. 205

Some years later, a Native American village grew in the area. 216
In the 1770s, settlers built a trading post. The spot was perfect 228
for the trading business, and more people arrived. 236

In the early 1800s, a fort was built near the town. The town 249
was now called Chicago. It grew into a small city. In 1848, 261
location paid off again. Trains that crossed the country began 271
passing through Chicago. A canal joined the two rivers. Chicago 281
was a center of transportation. More people moved there to earn 292
a living. 294

Trains brought other businesses to the city. One was 303
meatpacking. Trains carrying cattle and hogs roared into 311
Chicago. Other trains carried the meat out of the city. This 322
industry fed people all over the country. 329

Chicago became the center of catalog companies, too. People 338
from all over the world mailed in orders. Trains from Chicago 349
carried the orders to customers. Workers in Chicago made a 359
good living. 361

Chicago is also a center of aviation in the United States. 372
Its main airport is the busiest in the world. Airplanes bring 383
businesspeople from around the globe. 388

Today, millions of people live near the "Checagou" River. 397
A great location helped a small town grow into a great city. 409

Intervention

Using Your Cents

by David Grahm

It was Cindy's seventh birthday. Every year on her birthday, Cindy's grandparents gave her some money. She always looked forward to their gift.

"Buy yourself something special," they told her. "Enjoy it!"

Cindy never had trouble spending the money. She always went to Al's Toy Store. Al had a large selection of stuffed animals. He had stuffed bears, monkeys, sheep, birds, fish, and many other kinds of stuffed animals. Cindy planned to buy the one or two animals she liked most.

But this year was different. When Cindy arrived at Al's Toy Store, she wasn't excited to shop. Cindy entered the store and scanned the shelves. There were lots of stuffed animals, but she could not find any that she really liked. She wasn't sure what to do.

At last she thought, *I guess the little red foxes look okay.* She took two from the shelf and brought them to the front counter. Then she used her money to pay for them.

Cindy added the foxes to her collection, but she did not play   180
with them very much.   184

A few months later, Cindy was strolling by Al's Toy Store. She   196
saw some new stuffed animals in the window. There were baby   207
rabbits, deer, and mice.   211

Those babies are really cute! Cindy thought. *But I have no*   222
money to pay for them. Maybe I can make a trade.   233

She entered the store, and she talked to Al. "Hi, Al. Would it   246
be okay if I traded in my little red foxes for a new baby rabbit?"   261

"Sorry, Cindy," Al said, "but you bought the foxes awhile ago.   272
I can't let you trade them now for newer animals."   282

Later, Cindy told her parents her problem. She was really   292
disappointed. "I haven't played with my foxes much. So today   302
I asked Al if he would trade my foxes for a new baby rabbit, but   317
he said no," she told them.   323

"Why did you buy the foxes if you knew you would not play   336
with them?" asked Cindy's mom.   341

"I'm not sure," said Cindy. "I guess I wanted to spend the   353
birthday money Gramma and Grandpa gave me."   360

"Let this be a lesson," her father said. "You don't have to spend   373
all your money right away. Save it until you are sure of what   386
you want to buy. That makes good cents!"   394

Controlling Your Cash

by Gabrielle Fernandez

As you grow up, it's important to be smart with your money. First, you should make a budget. A budget is a way of tracking your money. It helps you decide what you need and want. It also helps you save.

A budget is a good idea for all people. Picture this. Alyssa is nine years old. Her parents give her $5.00 a week for helping around the house. Alyssa gets this allowance every Thursday night. But by Tuesday afternoon, Alyssa has no cash left for the rest of the week. She can't figure out where the money went!

Here are some simple steps Alyssa—and you—can follow.

Step One: What Are You Spending? People forget how they spent money. The best way to remember is to write down what you spend right away. Alyssa keeps a record of her spending for four weeks. She is surprised! Alyssa often uses some of her money for after-school snacks. But she didn't realize that she was spending almost $2.00 a week on snacks! She also spent money on some smaller toys she was collecting, nicer school supplies, renting movies, and baseball cards.

18
31
44
47

60
72
81
93
105

115

125
137
148
160
171
182
192
198

Step Two: What Is Important? After writing down how you spend your money, ask yourself some questions. Do you need everything you have purchased? Are there better ways to use your money? Do you want to save some of it? Do you want to help other people with it?

Alyssa thinks about her spending habits and decides she 256
doesn't need that many snacks. She also decides to save some 267
cash for gifts and other things. 273

Step Three: Make a Budget. Now you can make a spending 284
plan. How much money do you want to save? Will you spend 296
more or less money on games, toys, school supplies, or food? 307

This is Alyssa's weekly budget: 312

$1.00—put in a bank 317

$1.00—put in bedroom dresser drawer 323

$3.00—use first for school supplies and then a few snacks or 335
packs of baseball cards 339

Alyssa will use the money in the bank for buying important 350
things like a new bike, gifts, or a special trip. The money in her 364
drawer will be for once-in-a-while things like movies, toys, or 377
games. 378

Alyssa thinks of two other things. She remembers that 387
the local library lends movies for free. And she promises 397
herself that any extra money she receives—like cash from her 408
grandparents—will go into her bank or drawer. Alyssa is now a 420
better money manager. Now that you understand budgets, what 429
kind of budget will you make? 435

A Birthday Savings Plan

by Bob Swans

Maya was excited about her mother's upcoming birthday. 15
She planned to give her the most special gift. Maya had been 26
thinking about it since Mom's last birthday. 33

Maya had a big family. She had two older sisters and an older 46
brother. On Mom's birthday last year, each of the older kids had 58
given her a nice present. But Maya had not had enough money 70
for a gift. She had only given Mom a card she had made. 83

It was a very creative card. Maya drew a golden trophy on 95
it. On the trophy, she wrote, "World's Greatest Mother!" Mom 105
seemed to enjoy the card, too. But Maya felt bad. 115

The next day, Mom had shown Maya a big scrapbook she 126
kept in her desk. "I save important things in this scrapbook," she 138
explained. Maya flipped through the scrapbook. On page after 147
page, her mother had pasted cards from her and her siblings. 158
The book was almost full. 163

"I enjoy nice gifts," Mom said. "But the words and thoughts in 175
these cards are much more valuable." 181

Mom made Maya feel better. But she vowed that the next   192
year would be different. She would buy Mom something just like   203
everyone else did.   206

Maya had then asked her sister Ria how she could be   217
smarter about money. "Think about saving the moment you   226
get your allowance. Think about it when you get money from   237
Grandma," said Ria. "Then drop some of that money in your   248
piggy bank. Or ask Dad to help you open a savings account. If   261
you save a little every time, saving will become automatic. You'll 272
have enough cash for all kinds of gifts."   280

Maya had done exactly what Ria suggested. The year went by   291
and her savings had grown bigger. Now it was time to give Mom   304
the greatest birthday gift ever.   309

The next day Mom unwrapped her presents. She exclaimed   318
happily as she saw each one. Then Maya proudly handed Mom   329
her gift. It was a new scrapbook.   336

"This is such a thoughtful gift, Maya!" said Mom in a surprised   348
voice. "You remembered that my older scrapbook is almost full."   358

"And here's something else, Mom," Maya said, smiling. She   367
held up a beautiful birthday card she had made. "Buying the   378
scrapbook was fun, but it's the things in it that mean more."   390

"You are absolutely right, Maya," Mom said, as she placed the   401
card on the first clean, new page.   408

Team Spirit

by Darren Hearty

Miguel shook the can. A man had just dropped several
quarters into it. The coins made the loudest rattling noise.
"Great!" Miguel said.

"We'll need more," said Marta.

Twins Miguel and Marta were on the same baseball team.
The team needed new equipment. Well, really, the team had two
problems. It needed equipment and the money to buy it. That's
why the twins and their Aunt Rosa stood in front of the grocery
store with cans for coins. They were asking people to donate
loose change to help the team. The twins' teammates were at
other stores around Quincy doing the same thing.

The team's players, parents, and coaches worked hard to get the
money. They had several bake sales, car washes, and lemonade
stands, but they still needed more. That's why they sat behind their
donation cans instead of rounding the bases at the ballpark.

Miguel and Marta's Aunt Rosa was also the team's coach. At
the end of the longest day they could remember, the team met
at her house. The players emptied their cans on the table and
carefully counted everything.

The kids were excited. "Aunt Rosa," asked Miguel, "do you
think we have enough money to get the equipment?"

Aunt Rosa smiled. "You kids are the greatest. I believe we have enough," she said.   219
223

All the kids and parents cheered.   229

The next day a big story was in the news. The strongest   241
hurricane in history had moved up the coast. It had destroyed   252
homes and schools. It had left many, many people without   262
places to stay or food to eat.   269

Although the coast was far away from Quincy, the twins   279
were worried, but not about themselves. They worried about the   289
people whose lives were affected by the hurricane. Some people   299
lost everything—houses, furniture, cars, everything.   305

The twins quietly watched the news. "The people hurt by the   316
hurricane need a lot," said Marta. "We should use our baseball   327
equipment money to help them."   332

"I know," said Miguel.   336

They talked to Aunt Rosa and the other players on the team.   348
Aunt Rosa talked to the parents. Everyone agreed. The money   358
for the baseball equipment would be used to help the hurricane   369
victims.   370

That summer, the team used old equipment. The twins and   380
their teammates won quite a few games. But whether they won   391
or lost, they felt pretty good. They knew they had done the best   404
thing with their money.   408

Paco's Blankets

by Duncan Searl

Paco lived with his mother in a village in Guatemala. All year long, Mama worked at her loom, weaving the most colorful blankets. In the spring and summer, when the tourists came, Paco piled the stacks of blankets on the back of their mule. Then he carried them to the marketplace. "A gorgeous blanket, just 45 quetzals!" he called so tourists would come and take a closer look.

Other villagers were also weavers and sold blankets, too. "Only 40 quetzals for this blanket," Ramos called, "and it is just as beautiful!" Throughout the spring and summer, Paco and Ramos competed to sell blankets.

During the winter, disaster struck. A hurricane tore through Guatemala. It rained so hard that the earth on the mountain turned to mud. A wall of mud slid into the village. Hundreds of trees fell, and many buildings were knocked down. In the spring, there were no tourists.

17
27
38
51
61
73

82
94
103
108

117
128
141
152
156

"Where are the tourists?" Paco asked.   162

"The hurricane has made a mess of our village," his mother   173
explained. "Tourists will not keep coming here."   180

"How will we live if we cannot sell blankets?" Paco asked.   191
His mother just looked at the sky without answering. Paco   201
understood that she didn't have an answer to his question.   211

Then Paco had an idea. "If tourists won't come here," he   222
thought, "we can go to the tourists. Or at least our blankets can   235
go." Paco explained his idea to Brother Domingo. Domingo was   245
a teacher and had lived in the United States. He had the kindest   258
friends there.   260

Domingo organized a meeting with all the weavers. "My   269
friend will try to sell your blankets to stores in the United   281
States," Domingo said. "However, we will all have to cooperate."   291
At first, Paco and Ramos did not want to cooperate. They had   303
been competing for years to sell blankets. Cooperating with each   313
other was the strangest idea!   318

Soon, blankets began arriving at Domingo's school. A truck   327
carried them to Puerto Barrios, where the blankets were shipped   337
to the United States.   341

That summer, Paco, Ramos, and the other weavers did not go   352
to market. Instead, they cleaned up mud and rebuilt houses. By   363
fall, the village looked as good as new.   371

In the fall, the villagers were the   378
happiest they had been in years. All   385
their blankets had sold in the United   392
States! The weavers got 60 quetzals   398
for each blanket! Paco and Ramos   404
smiled at each other. "It pays to   411
cooperate!" they said.   414

Boffin Flea Market

by Angelica Thatcher

It was easy to get confused at Boffin Flea Market. The parking lot was always jammed with cars and bikes. Hundreds of people clogged the huge maze of small tents, vans, and booths where items were sold.

People could buy all kinds of things at the market: new and used clothes, fresh fruits and vegetables, grilled food, books, kitchenware, DVDs, CDs, jewelry, and on and on. Music played. People laughed and talked. The market was a jumble of colors, smells, and sounds.

Rachel was a regular at Boffin Flea Market. She loved the lively confusion. Her family had started selling things there years ago. Now Rachel knew all the vendors.

Every summer weekend, people came from faraway towns and cities to shop at the market. On those weekends, Boffin grew from a little town into a big one. The visitors spent money. That money helped the town.

Sometimes Rachel's family sold a lot at the flea market. Sometimes they didn't. Rachel and her big brother Lennie wanted to help Mom and Dad earn more. But how? Rachel and Lennie already worked at the family booth. But that didn't make the family more money.

17
27
38
43

55
64
74
85
88

99
108
116

124
135
148
153

163
172
184
195
199

During the first big summer weekend, Mom and Dad were   209
busy at the booth. Dad asked Rachel and Lennie to get some   221
things from the car. The car was parked in a faraway lot. As the 235
kids walked there, a man stopped them. He asked where he'd   246
find booths that sold old books.   252

As they walked farther, a boy asked Rachel if there were   263
booths that sold old postcards. And as Rachel and Lennie neared   274
the parking lot, some kids asked, "Where's the bratwurst stand?" 284

The parking lot was on a small hill. From the hill, Rachel and   297
Lennie could see all of Boffin Flea Market. "It looks like a map 310
of the market from up here," said Rachel. "And I've got a great   323
idea for helping the family earn more money."   331

Over the next week, Rachel and Lennie drew a detailed map   342
of Boffin Flea Market. They made hundreds of copies of it.   353

The next weekend, a new booth opened at the market. It   364
stood next to the parking lot. Across the top of the booth were   377
the words *Boffin Flea Market Map*. Rachel and Lennie stood in   388
the booth and sold copy after copy of the map. Rachel's idea had 401
paid off—in a big way!   407

Earning Money Can Be Fun!

by Tia Sanchez

"I'm frustrated," I said.

"How come?" asked my Uncle Jeff.

"I need to earn some money by next week, but I am running out of ideas."

"A penny saved is a penny earned," said Uncle Jeff.

"What good are pennies when I need twenty-five dollars?" I asked him.

Uncle Jeff chuckled. "You know, every penny you save adds up over time. And just why do you need twenty-five dollars?" he asked.

Uncle Jeff already knew the answer, but I told him anyway.

"I want to go to soccer camp next August," I said. "It's fifty dollars. Mom said I've got to earn half myself, but I am worried that I might not earn enough in time!"

"What have you been doing to earn money?" he asked.

I pulled a list out of my pocket and showed my uncle. "Well, well," he said. "You've been busy! Just last month you raked three lawns. You helped Mrs. Chen carry in groceries two times. And you cleaned your room every day!"

143
147
152
156
161
165
169
174
178

"I don't earn any money for cleaning my room," I said. "I wish I did!"

"How much money have you earned?" my uncle asked.

I added in my head as I answered Uncle Jeff. "I earned five dollars for each lawn I raked. I earned three dollars each time I carried groceries for Mrs. Chen. That's twenty-one dollars altogether."

215
227
237
238

"So you only need four more dollars! That's terrific!" Uncle Jeff said.

248
250

"Actually, I need five dollars," I replied. "I bought a new toy for Paws the other day."

262
267

Uncle Jeff didn't say much for a minute. He rubbed his chin like he always does when he's thinking about something. "I know how you can earn five dollars next week," said Uncle Jeff. "Are you interested?"

279
290
302
304

"I definitely am!" I said. I wondered if Uncle Jeff wanted me to do laundry or help him haul furniture. He didn't.

316
326

"I'm going to be gone a lot next week. Buster will be lonely. Could you take him for a walk after school every day?"

339
350

Could I ever! I adored Buster. Walking him was not going to feel like work. And besides that, at the end of the week, I'd have enough money for soccer camp! "Sure, Uncle Jeff! I would love to walk Buster. Thank you for offering!"

362
376
387
394

Earning money can be fun!

399

Name _____ **Date** _____

Focus

A **common noun** names any person, place, thing, or idea.
Examples: *girl, country, continent, magazine*
A **proper noun** names a certain person, place, thing, or idea.
Examples: *Kathy, Mexico, Asia, National Geographic*

Practice

Read each sentence. Underline the common nouns and circle the proper nouns.

1. Dr. Flynn works in a big hospital in San Diego.

2. My favorite movie is It's a Wonderful Life.

3. On Wednesday, our class is having a party to celebrate Thanksgiving.

4. Alaska, California, and Texas are the three largest states in the United States.

5. Claude Monet was one of the founding artists of Impressionism.

Apply

For each common noun, write a proper noun that could replace it.
Possible answers below.

	Common Noun	Proper Noun
1.	month	October
2.	school	Jefferson Elementary School
3.	song	"The Star-Spangled Banner"
4.	president	Abraham Lincoln
5.	book	"Island of the Blue Dolphins"

Name _____ Date _____

Focus

A **concrete noun** names something that you can see or touch.
An **abstract noun** names something you cannot see or touch.

Practice

Read each sentence. Underline the concrete nouns and circle the abstract nouns.

1. The <u>actor</u> seemed to have no (fear) on the <u>stage</u>.

2. The <u>teacher</u> asked his <u>students</u> to share their (thoughts.)

3. For (safety,) all the <u>players</u> wore <u>helmets</u>.

4. The (smell) of the <u>turkey</u> cooking made me so hungry!

5. The <u>coach</u> warned us about the (dangers) of too much (pride.)

Apply

Fill in the correct circle to tell whether each noun is concrete or abstract.

Noun	Concrete	Abstract
1. loneliness	○	●
2. planet	●	○
3. football	●	○
4. love	○	●
5. justice	○	●

Name _____ Date _____

Focus

Every complete sentence has at least one verb. A **verb** tells about the subject. It tells who the subject is or what the subject does.

Practice

Read each sentence. Circle the verbs.

1. Those students (are) in the fourth grade.

2. Jenny (finished) the race faster than I (did.)

3. Every night before bed, I (wash) my face and (brush) my teeth.

4. We (were) all sad when the song (ended.)

5. If you (study,) you (learn) more, and you (get) better grades.

Apply

Choose the correct verb from the Verb Bank to complete each sentence. Each verb will be used in only one sentence.

1. I _____ride_____ my bike to school.

2. My sister _____is_____ 15 years old.

3. The bird _____flies_____ high in the sky.

4. We _____talk_____ on the phone every day.

5. My grandparents _____live_____ in Florida.

6. The children _____jumped_____ up and down on the bed.

Verb Bank	
flies	is
jumped	live
ride	talk

Name _____ Date _____

Focus

Action verbs tell what the subject of a sentence does. Some action verbs express a physical action. Other action verbs express a mental action.

Practice

Circle the action verb in each sentence. In the blank, write *P* if the verb describes a physical action or *M* if the verb describes a mental action.

1. I (know) the capital of every state. __M__

2. The children (raced) after the basketball. __P__

3. (Look) at that sunset! __P__

4. I (guessed) the right answer in the trivia game! __M__

5. Mike slowly (opened) the door at the end of the hall. __P__

Apply

Fill in the correct circle to tell whether each action verb describes a physical action or a mental action.

Action Verb	Physical Action	Mental Action
1. carry	●	○
2. washed	●	○
3. imagine	○	●
4. stand	●	○
5. decided	○	●

Name _____ Date _____

Focus

Linking verbs express states of being. They connect the subject with a noun or adjective that renames or describes the subject.

Most linking verbs are a form of the verbs *to be, to seem,* or *to become.*

Practice

Circle the linking verb in each sentence.

1. I (am) a student at Jackson Elementary School.

2. Pepperoni (is) the best pizza topping.

3. Maria and Jamal (were) the winners.

4. (Are) you in the fourth grade?

5. My dog (seems) sad when I go to school.

Apply

Choose the correct linking verb to complete each sentence. Write the correct verb in the blank.

1. The dress _____is_____ red. (is/am)

2. My parents _____were_____ happy with my report card. (were/is)

3. It _____was_____ a great party! (be/was)

4. _____Be_____ nice to your sister! (Be/Is)

5. As the sun went down, it _____became_____ hard to see. (being/became)

6. Jane and Debbie _____are_____ my best friends. (be/are)

Name _____ Date _____

Focus

Helping verbs support the main verb in a sentence. There are 23 helping verbs: *am, are, is, was, were, be, being, been, do, does, did, have, has, had, may, must, might, can, could, will, would, shall, should.*

Practice

Circle the helping verbs in each sentence.

1. I (can) run really fast.

2. Tammy and Diego (are) playing checkers.

3. Devon (could) not find his backpack.

4. What (will) they eat for dinner?

5. The teacher (must have) seen us running in the halls.

Apply

Choose the correct helping verb to complete each sentence. Write the correct verb in the blank.

1. We really ____should____ get more exercise. (does/should)

2. My class ____is____ going on a field trip today. (will/is)

3. Karen ____had____ tried to explain how to do it many times. (had/could)

4. I told you I ____was____ here! (was/being)

5. The children ____were____ waiting to open the presents. (were/would)

6. I finished my report, but it ____might____ be too late. (did/might)

UNIT 1   **Lesson 4**

Name _____ Date _____

Focus

Nouns serve two main purposes in a sentence:

A **subject noun** does the action of the verb.

An **object noun** receives the action of the verb.

Practice

Read each sentence. Tell whether the underlined noun is a subject or an object. In the blank, write _S_ for subject or _O_ for object.

1. Mom cooked <u>hamburgers</u> for dinner. __O__

2. Our <u>teacher</u> gave out pencils on the first day of school. __S__

3. The <u>firefighter</u> hooked the hose to the hydrant. __S__

4. Danny mailed the <u>letter</u> to his grandmother. __O__

5. After studying for hours, <u>Max</u> got a high grade on the test. __S__

Apply

Write the subject noun and object noun in the correct blanks in each sentence.

1. A __bird__ built a __nest__ in the oak tree. (bird, nest)

2. The __carpenter__ hammered the __nails__ into the door. (nails, carpenter)

3. After every game, the __team__ sings our school __song__. (team, song)

4. The __president__ gave a __speech__ on television. (president, speech)

5. My __computer__ makes a funny __noise__ when I have mail. (noise, computer)

Name _____ Date _____

Focus

Pronouns replace nouns in sentences. A subject pronoun does the action of the verb. Subject pronouns: *I, it, he, she, you, we,* and *they.* An object pronoun receives the action of the verb. Object pronouns: *me, it, him, her, you, us,* and *them.*

Practice

Circle the pronoun in each sentence. In the blank, write *S* if the pronoun is a subject or *O* if it is an object.

1. The puppy licked (him) on the nose. ___O___

2. (We) drove all the way to Florida. ___S___

3. After lunch, (they) went for a walk. ___S___

4. If (you) want to go, then go. ___S___

Apply

Write the subject pronoun and object pronoun in the correct blanks in each sentence.

1. ___He___ called ___me___ this morning.

2. ___I___ told ___you___ to get here at eight!

3. ___They___ gave ___us___ a round of applause.

4. ___She___ followed ___them___ to school.

Pronouns	
he	me
you	I
us	they
them	she

Name _____ Date _____

> # Focus
> Sentences have two main parts—a subject and a predicate.
>   The **simple subject** is the noun or pronoun that the sentence is about.
>   A **simple predicate** is the main verb or verb phrase of the sentence.

Practice

Read each sentence. Underline the simple subject and circle the simple predicate.

1. We (walk) to school together every morning.

2. Jamie (lives) in San Francisco.

3. All the books (are arranged) in alphabetical order.

4. In autumn, the leaves (turn) orange and red.

5. The player wearing the striped shirt is the goalie.

Apply

**Identify the simple subject and predicate of each sentence.
Write each in the correct blank.**

1. The airplane landed fifteen minutes late.

   simple subject: ___airplane___ **simple predicate:** ___landed___

2. Emily has a guitar lesson every Thursday.

   simple subject: ___Emily___ **simple predicate:** ___has___

3. You should listen to this new song.

   simple subject: ___you___ **simple predicate:** ___should listen___

Name _____ Date _____

Focus

The **complete subject** of a sentence is the simple subject and all of its modifiers. A **complete predicate** of a sentence is the simple predicate and all of its modifiers.

Practice

Read each sentence. Underline the complete subject and circle the complete predicate.

1. The girl walked.

2. The girl walked slowly.

3. The tired girl walked slowly.

4. The tired girl walked slowly up the hill.

5. The tired girl in the blue dress walked slowly up the hill.

Apply

Decide whether the underlined part of each sentence is part of the complete subject or the complete predicate. In the blank, write **S** for complete subject or **P** for complete predicate.

1. You have to feed your fish <u>everyday</u>.   P

2. Our next-door <u>neighbors</u> are selling their house.   S

3. Mrs. Davis loves to go <u>shopping</u> at the mall.   P

4. I did <u>a lot</u> of chores this weekend.   P

5. On Friday, <u>our</u> class is going to the aquarium.   S

Name _____ **Date** _____

Focus

A complete simple sentence has:
- one subject and one predicate.
- a capitalized first letter.
- end punctuation, such as a period or question mark.

Practice

The sentences below are incomplete. Tell whether each is missing a subject or a predicate.

1. Visited my grandmother and grandfather. _____ missing subject _____

2. The book "The Snowflake: A Water Cycle Story." _____ missing predicate _____

3. On Saturday, played basketball for two hours. _____ missing subject _____

4. Joyfully skipped on the playground. _____ missing subject _____

5. Every year on New Year's Eve my friends and I. _____ missing predicate _____

Apply

Fill in the correct circle to tell whether each simple sentence is complete or incomplete.

Simple Sentence	Complete	Incomplete
1. Driving down the highway.	○	●
2. The blue sweater is pretty.	●	○
3. Every fourth-grader in school.	○	●
4. Quickly ran to the grocery store.	○	●
5. Dancing can be fun.	●	○

Name _____ Date _____

Focus

A noun or pronoun can be an object of a sentence in two ways:
It is the **direct object** if it receives the action of the verb.
It is the **object of a preposition** when it is at the end of a prepositional phrase.

Practice

Circle the object noun or pronoun in each sentence. Then tell if it is a direct object or an object of a preposition.

1. The quarterback threw the (football). _____ direct object _____

2. Jennifer spoke to (him). _____ object of a preposition _____

3. We ate before the (movie). _____ object of a preposition _____

4. He read (it) very fast. _____ direct object _____

5. The kids jumped on the (bed). _____ object of a preposition _____

Apply

Tell if each underlined noun or pronoun is a direct object or an object of a preposition. In the blank, write *DO* for direct object or *OP* for object of a preposition.

1. My brother watched the <u>movie</u> three times! ___ DO ___

2. We saw <u>them</u> in the show. ___ DO ___

3. The plane flew over the <u>mountains</u>. ___ OP ___

4. All the puppies ran to <u>her</u>. ___ OP ___

5. They paddled the <u>canoe</u> across the river. ___ DO ___

Name _____ **Date** _____

Focus
A **declarative sentence** makes a statement and gives information.
An **exclamatory sentence** expresses strong emotion.
An **interrogative sentence** asks a question.
An **imperative sentence** makes a request or gives a command.

Practice
Circle the end mark in each sentence and identify the type of sentence.

1. That movie was awesome! ___exclamatory___

2. My brother is 16 years old. ___declarative___

3. How do I get to Main Street? ___interrogative___

4. Don't open that door! ___imperative___

Apply
Identify each sentence type. Then write your own example of each type.
Possible answers below.

1. Give the book to me.   imperative _____

   Clean your room. _____

2. Sacramento is the capital of California.   declarative _____

   His cooking is better than hers. _____

3. We're getting married!   exclamatory _____

   I won the lottery! _____

4. Why are you late?   interrogative _____

   Can I come too? _____

Name _____ Date _____

Focus

Quotation marks are used for dialogue, quotations, and titles of short works, such as poems or stories.

- In dialogue, end marks usually go inside the quotation marks.
- When the sentence, not the dialogue, asks a question, the question mark goes outside the quotation marks.

Practice

Place quotation marks around the correct text in each sentence.

1. Mr. Samuels said, "You will have a quiz tomorrow."

2. The police officer asked, "Do you need help?"

3. The coach screamed, "Get back on defense!"

4. Our teacher read a new selection called "What's Ecology?"

5. Have you read the poem "The Road Less Traveled"?

Apply

Complete each sentence by writing appropriate text in quotation marks.
Possible answers below.

1. My favorite story is "The Great Kapok Tree." _____

2. My teacher said, "Do your homework!" _____

3. The cook asked, "Do you like hamburgers?" _____

4. My best friend shouted, "Look out!" _____

5. My mom always says, "Call me when you get there." _____

Name _____ **Date** _____

Focus

A sentence with a **compound subject** has more than one subject.

Practice

Underline the compound subject in each sentence.

1. <u>Students and teachers</u> will attend the assembly.

2. <u>The yellow daisies and orange tulips</u> look pretty together.

3. On Monday, <u>Brenda and Leroy</u> were late to school.

Apply

Rewrite each sentence so that it has a compound subject.

Possible answers below.

1. Soccer is my favorite sport.

   Soccer and basketball are my favorite sports.

2. The cars sped along the highway.

   The cars and trucks sped along the highway.

3. Roses grow in the garden.

   Roses and lilies grow in the garden.

4. My aunt sent me a birthday present.

   My aunt and uncle sent me a birthday present.

5. Reading is fun on a rainy afternoon.

   Reading and watching movies are fun on a rainy afternoon.

Name _____ Date _____

Focus

A sentence with a **compound object** has more than one object.
It can be a compound direct object or a compound object of a preposition.

Practice

Underline the compound object in each sentence. Tell whether each is a compound direct object or a compound object of a preposition.

1. I gave my notes to <u>Tim and Anita</u>. compound object of a preposition

2. We ordered <u>soup and salad</u> for lunch. compound direct object

3. They visited <u>Portland and Seattle</u>. compound direct object

Apply

Rewrite each sentence so that is has a compound object.
Possible answers below.

1. The bird flew over the river.

   The bird flew over the river and lake.

2. I like to wear jeans to school.

   I like to wear sweaters and jeans to school.

3. The leaves turn brown in October.

   The leaves turn brown in October and November.

4. I ate hot dogs at the baseball game.

   I ate hot dogs and peanuts at the baseball game.

Name _____ Date _____

> # Focus
> A sentence with a **compound predicate** has more than one predicate—two or more verbs share the same subject.

Practice

Underline the compound predicate in each sentence.

1. Lions <u>hunt</u> and <u>sleep</u> all day.

2. The sun <u>looks</u> bright and <u>feels</u> warm.

3. The dog <u>jumped</u> into the lake and <u>chased</u> the duck.

Apply

Rewrite each sentence so that it has a compound predicate.
Possible answers below.

1. I swam at the beach.

   I swam and surfed at the beach.

2. The squirrel ran across the yard.

   The squirrel ran across the yard and climbed up a tree.

3. Mr. Jones cooked all day.

   Mr. Jones cooked and cleaned all day.

4. The carpenter cut the wood.

   The carpenter cut and sanded the wood.

5. We shopped at the mall.

   We shopped and ate lunch at the mall.

Name _____ **Date** _____

Focus

Three uses for **commas** are:
- separating subjects, objects, or predicates in a series.
- separating elements in dates.
- separating elements in addresses.

Practice

Place the comma or commas where needed in each sentence.

1. My birthday is December 5, 1989.

2. Emily, Megan, and Consuela are best friends.

3. The company is based in Miami, Florida.

4. He speaks French, Spanish, and English.

5. Mr. Samuels planted, weeded, and watered the garden.

Apply

Place the comma or commas where needed in the following sentences. Circle any commas that should be deleted. If the commas are placed correctly in the sentence, place a check mark at the end.

1. You can swim, boat, and, fish, at the lake.

2. We took a train to Seattle, Washington. ✓

3. California, Arizona, New Mexico, and Texas border, Mexico.

4. Chimpanzees eat fruit, plants, seeds, and, insects.

5. The Civil War started on April 12, 1861.

Name _____ Date _____

Focus

A **conjunction** is a word that connects parts of a sentence.
Coordinating conjunctions (*and, or, but, for, nor, yet, so*) join like elements in sentences, such as subject + subject.

Practice

Circle the conjunction in each sentence.

1. The dog was happy, (so) he wagged his tail.

2. I made a sandwich with turkey (and) cheese.

3. He rushed to get there, (but) he was still late.

4. We could play a game (or) go for a walk.

5. I have not met him, (nor) do I want to.

Apply

Write an appropriate coordinating conjunction in each blank to complete the sentence.

1. We practiced dribbling __and__ shooting baskets.

2. The electricity was out, __so__ we had to eat in the dark.

3. Do you play the guitar __or__ the bass?

4. I bought a new map, __for__ I did not want to get lost.

5. She got the package, __but/yet__ she did not open it.

Name _____ **Date** _____

Focus

A **compound sentence** is formed by joining two or more simple sentences with a comma and a conjunction.

Practice

Write the two simple sentences that form each compound sentence.

1. The stem is rough, but the leaves are soft.

The stem is rough. The leaves are soft.

2. I missed the bus, so I was late to school.

I missed the bus. I was late to school.

3. The fork goes on the left, and the knife goes on the right.

The fork goes on the left. The knife goes on the right.

Apply

Combine each pair of simple sentences to form one compound sentence.

1. His pants are brown. His shirt is blue.

His pants are brown, and his shirt is blue.

2. I want to bake a pie. I don't know how.

I want to bake a pie, but I don't know how.

3. Do you want to go bowling? Do you want to see a movie?

Do you want to go bowling, or do you want to see a movie?

Name _____ **Date** _____

Focus

A **possessive noun** tells who or what owns or has something.
Add an apostrophe (') and an s to make most singular nouns possessive.
Add only an apostrophe to make most plural nouns possessive.

Practice

Circle the possessive noun and tell if it is a singular or plural.

1. We're having dinner at (Robert's) house tonight. _____ singular _____

2. The (mayor's) speech was very long. _____ singular _____

3. All of the (volunteers') efforts were a success. _____ plural _____

4. The (officers') uniforms are dark blue. _____ plural _____

Apply

Choose the correct possessive noun to complete each sentence.

1. My ___brother's___ bicycle has a flat tire.
   a. brother's   **b.** brothers's   **c.** brothers

2. That ___bird's___ nest is on the highest branch.
   a. birds   **b.** birds'   **c.** bird's

3. Both ___workers'___ tools are locked in the shed.
   a. workers'   **b.** workers's   **c.** worker's

4. The ___winner's___ medal is gold.
   a. winners's   **b.** winners   **c.** winner's

5. The teacher graded all of her ___students'___ tests.
   a. students   **b.** students'   **c.** student's

Name _____ **Date** _____

Focus

A **subjective pronoun** replaces a subject in a sentence.
An **objective pronoun** replaces an object in a sentence.
A **possessive pronoun** replaces a possessive noun in a sentence.

Practice

Circle the pronoun and tell if it is subjective, objective, or possessive.

1. (They) ate lunch together. ___subjective___

2. Amy's shirt is red, but (mine) is blue. ___possessive___

3. The coach told (you) not to be late. ___objective___

4. Mom gave (us) extra money to buy popcorn at the movies. ___objective___

5. Karen and (I) went shopping yesterday. ___subjective___

Apply

Choose the correct pronoun to complete each sentence.

1. Maggie invited ___them___ to the party.
   a. they   **b.** theirs   **c.** them

2. ___We___ laughed through the whole movie.
   a. We   **b.** Us   **c.** Ours

3. Jamal forwarded the e-mail to ___me___.
   a. I   **b.** me   **c.** mine

4. If that is your phone ringing, then answer ___it___.
   a. it   **b.** its   **c.** it's

5. I gave Brad my address and he gave me ___his___.
   a. him   **b.** his   **c.** her

Name _____ Date _____

Focus

Relative pronouns relate a clause to the noun it describes in a sentence. The main relative pronouns are *that, which, who, whom,* and *whose.*

Practice

Circle the relative pronoun in each sentence. Identify the noun that it relates to in the sentence.

1. The poem (that) she wrote won an award. _____ poem _____

2. The car, (which) was red, sped through the intersection. _____ car _____

3. The man (whose) house is for rent called today. _____ man _____

4. Children (who) do not wear helmets cannot enter the race. _____ Children _____

5. I saw some people at the party (whom) I had met before. _____ people _____

Apply

Choose the correct relative pronoun to complete each sentence.

1. Cats _____ that _____ like dogs are unusual.
   a. that   **b.** whose   **c.** whom

2. The boys _____ who _____ skateboard at the mall are noisy.
   a. whose   **b.** that   **c.** who

3. Someone, _____ whose _____ name I forget, called you today.
   a. that   **b.** whose   **c.** which

4. The snow _____ that _____ fell all night covered the roads.
   a. that   **b.** which   **c.** whose

5. The guide with _____ whom _____ we traveled was very friendly.
   a. that   **b.** whose   **c.** whom

Name _____ **Date** _____

Focus

Demonstrative pronouns replace nouns that must be pointed to. The main demonstrative pronouns are *this, that, these,* and *those. This* and *that* are singular, and *these* and *those* are plural.

Practice

Circle the demonstrative pronoun in each sentence. Tell if each is singular or plural.

1. (That) is a great idea! _____ singular

2. (These) will look great in my kitchen. _____ plural

3. How much does (this) cost? _____ singular

4. (Those) are the shoes I want. _____ plural

5. Did you see (that?) _____ singular

Apply

Tell if *this, that, these,* or *those* acts as a demonstrative pronoun or a demonstrative adjective in each sentence. In the blank, write *pronoun* or *adjective.*

1. This street will take you downtown. _____ adjective

2. Those look great with your hair color. _____ pronoun

3. I hope this doesn't bother you. _____ pronoun

4. We bought these at the farmers market. _____ pronoun

5. That boy is always causing trouble. _____ adjective

Name _____ Date _____

Focus

Superlative adjectives compare three or more things. To create most one-syllable superlative adjectives, add *-est*. For many adjectives with two or more syllables, only add the word *most* before the adjective.

Practice

Change the adjectives below to their superlative form by either adding *-est* or using the word *most*.

1. bright _____brightest_____

2. loving _____most loving_____

3. great _____greatest_____

4. annoying _____most annoying_____

Apply

Choose the correct superlative adjective to complete each sentence.

1. Jeremy was the _____fastest_____ runner on the team.
  a. fast   **b.** most fast   **c.** fastest

2. Paul is the _most creative_ person I know.
  a. most creative   **b.** creativest   **c.** creativer

3. My grandmother is the _____wisest_____ person in my family.
  a. wisest   **b.** wise   **c.** most wise

4. Our day at the zoo was the _most exciting_ field trip this year.
  a. exciting   **b.** most exciting   **c.** excitingest

Name _____ **Date** _____

Focus

Superlative adjectives compare three or more things. Irregular superlative adjectives are not formed by adding -*est* or the word *most*. Instead, these adjectives must be memorized. Examples include *good, well, best; bad, worst; many, much, most; little, least.*

Practice

Match the adjective with its correct irregular superlative form.

1. good   **a.** worst

2. little   **b.** most

3. much   **c.** least

4. bad   **d.** best

Apply

Choose the correct irregular superlative adjective for the sentences below.

1. Allison is the ____most____ qualified person for the job.
   a. more   **b.** most   **c.** mostest

2. Bryan and Valerie have been ____best____ friends for many years.
   a. best   **b.** most good   **c.** better

3. Lisa scored the ____least____ number of points in the game.
   a. lest   **b.** most little   **c.** least

4. Susan said, "That was the ____worst____ show I have ever seen!"
   a. baddest   **b.** worst   **c.** worser

Name _____ Date _____

Focus

Rules for changing **regular adjectives** to their comparative forms:
If the adjective has one syllable, add the *-er* suffix.
If it has three or more syllables, say "more" before the adjective.
If it has two syllables, either add *-er* or say "more."

Practice

Choose the correct comparative adjective to complete each sentence.

1. Antwan is _____shorter_____ than Melissa.
   a. shorter   **b.** more shortest

2. Yesterday was _____colder_____ than it is today.
   a. colder   **b.** more cold

3. Your chair is _____more comfortable_____ than mine.
   a. comfortabler   **b.** more comfortable

4. The last math problem was _____more difficult_____ than the rest.
   a. more difficult   **b.** difficulter

5. My new book is _____funnier_____ than the one I just read.
   a. more funny   **b.** funnier

Apply

Complete the chart by writing the comparative form of each regular adjective.

	Adjective	Comparative
1.	dark	darker
2.	delicious	more delicious
3.	happy	happier
4.	rich	richer
5.	important	more important

Name _____ **Date** _____

Focus

Irregular adjectives have unique comparative forms.
You do not add -er to the end of the adjective.
You do not say "more" before the adjective.

Practice

Choose the correct comparative adjective to complete each sentence.

1. Alaska is ___farther___ north than California.
   a. farther   **b.** farrer

2. I feel ___worse___ today than I did yesterday.
   a. worser   **b.** worse

3. Jamie's music is ___better___ than mine.
   a. more good   **b.** better

4. My cat weighs ___less___ than my dog.
   a. less   **b.** lesser

5. Brent sold ___more___ cookies than any other student.
   a. much   **b.** more

Apply

Complete the chart by writing the comparative form of each irregular adjective.

	Adjective	Comparative
1.	bad	worse
2.	many	more
3.	good	better
4.	far	farther
5.	little	less

Name _____ Date _____

Focus

Adverbs modify a verb, adjective, or another adverb. They tell how, when, or where something is done.
Some adverbs can also be adjectives.
Most adverbs are adjectives with the *-ly* suffix added.

Practice

Circle the adverb in each sentence.

1. We (rarely) see that kind of bird in our area.

2. Darnell is (extremely) smart.

3. Their plane arrived (early.)

4. She sang (softly.)

5. I (immediately) called the police.

Apply

For each sentence, tell if the underlined word is used as an adjective or an adverb. Write *adjective* or *adverb* in the blank.

1. She woke up <u>late</u> this morning.   _____adverb_____

2. Our bus driver loves <u>fast</u> cars.   _____adjective_____

3. I think I did <u>badly</u> on the test.   _____adverb_____

4. He hit the nail <u>hard</u> with his hammer.   _____adverb_____

5. I bought the <u>daily</u> newspaper.   _____adjective_____

Name _____ **Date** _____

Focus

Rules for changing **adverbs** to their comparative and superlative forms:
- If the adverb can also be an adjective, add the *-er* and *-est* suffix.
- If the adverb ends in the suffix *-ly*, use "more" and "most" before it.
- If it is an irregular adverb, use its unique comparative or superlative.

Practice

Choose the correct comparative or superlative adverb to complete each sentence.

1. I'll try ____harder____ on the next test.
   a. harder   **b.** hard

2. Katie ran ___the fastest___ of all the students in her class.
   a. faster   **b.** the fastest

3. You were ____faster____ than him.
   a. faster   **b.** fastest

4. Our teacher asked us to work _more quietly_.
   a. more quiet   **b.** more quietly

Apply

Complete the chart by writing the comparative or superlative form of each adverb.

	Adverb	Comparative	Superlative
1.	badly	worse	worst
2.	early	earlier	earliest
3.	clearly	more clearly	most clearly
4.	loudly	more loudly	most loudly
5.	well	better	best

Name _____ **Date** _____

> # Focus
> To form the **present tense** of a regular verb, add the -s or -es ending for *he, she,* and other singular subjects (except *I* and *you*).
> To form the **past tense** of a regular verb, add the -ed ending for all subjects.

Practice
Choose the correct verb to complete each sentence and write it on the line.

1. Tammy and Latoya __walk__ to school together.
   a. walk   **b.** walks

2. It __rained__ for hours yesterday.
   a. rained   **b.** rain

3. My sister __hates__ spiders.
   a. hates   **b.** hate

4. I __watched__ a great movie last night.
   a. watch   **b.** watched

Apply
Circle the verb in each sentence. On the line, write if the verb is *present tense* or *past tense.*

1. Jennifer (collects) stamps from around the world. _____ present tense _____

2. I (dropped) the letter in the mailbox. _____ past tense _____

3. Ben and Paco (share) a locker. _____ present tense _____

4. The hiker (carried) water in her backpack. _____ past tense _____

5. The train (arrived) at noon. _____ past tense _____

Name _____ **Date** _____

Focus

An **irregular verb** is a verb that does not follow the rule for adding –ed to form the past tense of the verb. Each verb has its own spelling changes and forms.

Practice

Circle the correct past tense form for each irregular verb.

1. drink   **a.** drinked   **b.** (drank)

2. go   **a.** (went)   **b.** goed

3. speak   **a.** speaked   **b.** (spoke)

4. make   **a.** (made)   **b.** maked

5. fly   **a.** (flew)   **b.** flied

Apply

Write in the correct past tense form of each irregular verb for each sentence.

1. I _____forgot_____ my book bag at school today. (forget)

2. The boy _____wrote_____ a letter to his pen pal. (write)

3. Sabrina _____sat_____ under the bridge, waiting for the rain to stop. (sit)

4. Our school's soccer team _____won_____ the championship game. (win)

5. Michael _____caught_____ his first fly ball today at practice. (catch)

Name _____ **Date** _____

Focus

The verb **to be** has unique present and past tense forms:
Present Tense: *I am, He/She/It is, You/We/They are.*
Past Tense: *I/He/She/It was, You/We/They were.*

Practice

Circle the form of the verb *to be* in each sentence. On the line, write if the form is *present tense* or *past tense* and *singular* or *plural*.

1. We (were) so happy at the park. _____ past tense, plural _____

2. I (am) in the fourth grade. _____ present, singular _____

3. She (was) afraid of the dark. _____ past, singular _____

4. The dog and cat (are) friends. _____ present, plural _____

Apply

Circle the correct form of *to be* to complete each sentence.

1. I _____ so sad when the movie ended.
  a. (was)   **b.** is

2. Henry _____ a good dancer.
  a. (is)   **b.** am

3. My parents _____ downstairs in the living room.
  a. was   **b.** (are)

4. The kids _____ outside all day.
  a. was   **b.** (were)

5. On most days I _____ glad to go to school.
  a. (am)   **b.** are

Name _____ **Date** _____

Focus

The past tense forms of **irregular verbs** are not formed by the *-ed* suffix.
Some have the same present and past tense form.
Some keep the initial consonant(s) and add *-ought* or *-aught*.
Some change *i* to *a*.
Others have unique past tenses.

Practice

Circle the correct past tense form for each irregular verb.

1. catch   **a.** catched   **b.** (caught)

2. sit   **a.** (sat)   **b.** set

3. break   **a.** (broke)   **b.** brake

4. fall   **a.** fall   **b.** (fell)

5. hit   **a.** (hit)   **b.** hitted

Apply

Circle the irregular verb in each sentence. On the line, write if the verb is *present tense* **or** *past tense.*

1. I (wrote) a letter to my best friend. _____ past _____

2. Cindy (eats) cereal for breakfast. _____ present _____

3. My dad (got) a parking ticket. _____ past _____

4. Mrs. Jackson (teaches) art. _____ present _____

5. The choir (sang) a new song. _____ past _____

Name _____ **Date** _____

Focus
In every sentence, the **verb** must agree in number with its **subject**.

Practice
For each sentence, circle the verb that agrees with its subject.

1. Tony _____ a great singer.
   a. (is)   **b.** am

2. I _____ the books on the shelves.
   a. (put)   **b.** puts

3. We _____ pizza for dinner.
   a. (cook)   **b.** cooks

4. Jenny _____ her coach at the mall.
   a. see   **b.** (sees)

Apply
Correct each sentence by changing the verb so it agrees with its subject.

1. Samantha <u>ride</u> the bus to school. _____ rides _____

2. The players <u>wants</u> a new coach. _____ want _____

3. Cats <u>is</u> good at landing on their feet. _____ are _____

4. I <u>lives</u> two blocks from the beach. _____ live _____

Name _____ **Date** _____

Focus

Commas separate items in series, dates, and addresses.

Practice

Write a comma or commas in the correct places in each sentence.

1. My best friend lives in Chicago, Illinois.

2. Emily, Emma, and Abigail were the most popular names for girls this year.

3. Americans declared independence from Britain on July 4, 1776.

Apply

Rewrite each sentence so it needs a comma in a series, date, or address.
Possible answers below.

1. Tim's birthday is in June.

   Tim's birthday is June 1, 1998.

2. I saw lions and elephants at the zoo.

   I saw lions, elephants, and zebras at the zoo.

3. Juan lives in California.

   Juan lives in Los Angeles, California.

4. We ate lunch and saw a movie at the mall.

   We ate lunch, saw a movie, and shopped at the mall.

5. Seattle has a rainy climate.

   Seattle, Washington, has a rainy climate.

Name _____ Date _____

Focus

Some sentences have a **compound subject**, or more than one subject that shares the same predicate.

Practice

For each sentence, underline the compound subject and circle the verb the subjects share.

1. Laura and Emilio (live) in Texas.

2. Yellow daisies, white lilies, and pink tulips (are) in the vase.

3. California, Washington, and Oregon (border) the Pacific Ocean.

4. Tanya, Sam, Niko, and Will (sit) at the same table.

Apply

Rewrite each sentence so it has a compound subject. Possible answers below.

1. Blue is my favorite color.

   Blue and green are my favorite colors.

2. Puppies are cute.

   Puppies and kittens are cute.

3. The dresses hang in the closet.

   The dresses, shirts, and suits hang in the closet.

4. I went to the beach.

   My parents and I went to the beach.

Name _____ **Date** _____

Focus

Some sentences have a **compound predicate**, or more than one predicate that shares the same subject.

Practice

For each sentence, underline the verbs in the compound predicate and circle the subject the predicates share.

1. (Mr. Jackson) <u>lives</u> in the suburbs and <u>works</u> in the city.

2. The (dog) <u>dug</u> a hole and <u>buried</u> his bone.

3. (Amy) <u>brushed</u> her teeth and <u>washed</u> her face.

4. The (teacher) <u>says</u> each word and <u>uses</u> it in a sentence.

5. (Toby) <u>speaks</u>, <u>reads</u>, and <u>writes</u> three languages.

Apply

Rewrite each sentence so it has a compound predicate. Possible answers below.

1. We ate breakfast.

   We ate breakfast and drank milk.

2. She kicked the ball.

   She kicked the ball and scored a goal.

3. Ted opens the door.

   Ted opens the door and walks outside.

4. The cat jumps on the counter.

   The cat jumps on the counter and licks the milk.

Name _____ Date _____

Focus

A sentence is a **fragment** if it is missing a subject or a predicate.
A sentence is a **run-on** if it contains more than one thought that should be expressed in two or more shorter sentences.

Practice

Rewrite each sentence to correct the fragment or run-on. Possible answers below.

1. The sun is strong put on more sunscreen.

   The sun is strong. Put on more sunscreen.

2. Raining all day.

   It has been raining all day.

3. The bakery sells great pies I like the apple pie best

   The bakery sells great pies. I like the apple pie best.

Apply

Identify if each sentence is a *fragment* or a *run-on*. Then correct the sentence. Possible answers below.

1. We drove to Florida the road was crowded. _____run-on_____

   We drove to Florida. The road was crowded.

2. Tabitha and her older brother Rick. _____fragment_____

   Tabitha and her older brother Rick won the contest.

3. Quickly grabbed my backpack and ran to catch the bus. _____fragment_____

   I quickly grabbed my backpack and ran to catch the bus.

Name _____ **Date** _____

Focus

Present tense verbs describe actions that are taking place now.
Past tense verbs describe actions that already took place.
Future tense verbs describe actions that will take place later.

Practice

Circle the verb in each sentence and tell if it is in *present, past,* or *future* tense.

1. I (will finish) my work when I get home. _____ future _____

2. Everyone (laughed) at my joke. _____ past _____

3. The trucks (drive) in the fast lane. _____ present _____

4. My mom (made) pancakes for breakfast. _____ past _____

5. The team (will practice) harder. _____ future _____

Apply

Complete the chart by writing the correct present, past, or future tense of each verb with the given subject.

	Present	**Past**	**Future**
1.	She sits.	She sat.	She will sit.
2.	They dance.	They danced.	They will dance.
3.	I study.	I studied.	I will study.
4.	We are.	We were.	We will be.
5.	You smile.	You smiled.	You will smile.

Name _____ **Date** _____

Focus

A **preposition** is a word that relates a noun, pronoun, or group of words to another word in a sentence. Prepositions usually indicate relationships of time or place.

The most commonly used prepositions are: *of, in, to, with, as, at, for, on, by,* and *from.*

Practice

Underline the preposition in each sentence.

1. The train leaves <u>at</u> noon.

2. The apartment <u>below</u> mine is empty.

3. Your project must be done <u>by</u> Friday.

4. The flowers <u>in</u> the garden are blooming.

5. Please keep your feet <u>off</u> the table.

Apply

Complete each sentence with an appropriate preposition.

1. The girl _____with_____ the red umbrella is my sister.

2. Always eat breakfast _____before_____ school.

3. The Johnsons live _____in_____ San Diego, California.

4. My legs do not fit _____under_____ this small desk.

5. What present did you make _____for_____ your father?

Name _____ Date _____

Focus

A **prepositional phrase** consists of a preposition, its object, and any modifiers of that object.

Prepositional phrases act like adjectives or adverbs: They modify a noun or verb in the sentence.

down   the   hill

preposition   modifier   object

Practice

Underline the prepositional phrase in each sentence.

1. It often rains in the summer.

2. The store is closed on Mondays.

3. Some people talked during the movie.

4. The main character of the story is a dragon.

5. Sharon got a new dress for her birthday.

Apply

Underline the prepositional phrase in each sentence. Then write the noun or verb that the prepositional phrase modifies.

1. The picnic in the park was fun. _____ picnic _____

2. I bought a bag of popcorn. _____ bag _____

3. Nathan studies after school. _____ studies _____

4. The cat hides under the couch. _____ hides _____

5. We ride our bikes behind the school. _____ ride _____

Name _____ **Date** _____

Focus

The **object of a preposition** is the noun or pronoun that follows a preposition in a prepositional phrase.

Practice

Circle the object of the preposition in each sentence.

1. Money doesn't grow on (trees).

2. Jane's birthday is in (June).

3. Phil went to the (store).

4. The dog under the (table) is hungry.

5. Which color in this (picture) do you like best?

Apply

Underline the prepositional phrase in each sentence. Then tell the object of the preposition.

1. Ben found a five-dollar bill on the street. _____ street _____

2. I promise to send the package by Monday. _____ Monday _____

3. We haven't seen you since last year. _____ year _____

4. Please write your name above the date. _____ date _____

5. The letter from Wendy is so funny. _____ Wendy _____

Name _____ **Date** _____

Focus

An **object of a preposition** can be a noun or a pronoun.
These are the pronouns that can be objects of a preposition:
me, him, her, it, you, us, and them.

Practice

Circle the pronoun that is the object of the preposition in each sentence.

1. Tony gave his old books to (me).

2. I'll hold the umbrella over (you).

3. The present for (them) is wrapped.

4. Put the napkins and silverware on (it).

5. That girl keeps staring at (us).

Apply

Rewrite each sentence by using the correct pronoun to replace the noun that is the object of the preposition.

1. Hilary sang with Antwan. Hilary sang with him. _____

2. The students hung the sign over the door. The students hung the sign over it. _____

3. That dog belongs to Rita and Sam. That dog belongs to them. _____

4. The boy with Lisa won the spelling bee. The boy with her won the spelling bee. _____

5. The star of the play is very talented. The star of it is very talented. _____

Name _____ Date _____

Focus

Sometimes you can **combine two sentences** by placing some of the information in a prepositional phrase.

Practice

Underline the prepositional phrase in each sentence.

1. The dog <u>with the white spots</u> is named Casey.

2. <u>Of all the swimmers on the team</u>, Paco is the fastest.

3. He tried to get some work done <u>during the train ride</u>.

4. That girl <u>across the street</u> is my best friend.

Apply

Complete each sentence so that it combines the two sentences above it with a prepositional phrase.

1. The light is broken. The light is over the kitchen table.

   The light ____<u>over the kitchen table</u>____ is broken

2. The tree is growing. The tree is behind my house.

   The tree _____<u>behind my house</u>_____ is growing.

3. The test will be hard. The test is on Friday.

   The test _____<u>on Friday</u>_____ will be hard.

4. My extra sweaters are in a box. The box is under my bed.

   My extra sweaters are in a box _____<u>under my bed.</u>_____

Name _____ **Date** _____

Focus

An **appositive** is a noun that is placed next to another noun to identify it or to add more information. An **appositive phrase** is a group of words that includes an appositive and words that describe the appositive. Appositive phrases can combine two sentences into one.

Practice

Underline the appositive or appositive phrase in each of the following sentences.

1. Tony's uncle made spaghetti, <u>his favorite meal</u>, for dinner last night.

2. My cousins, <u>Matt and Dan</u>, always make me laugh.

3. Elizabeth's mother, <u>the school librarian</u>, told me not to run in the hallway.

4. George, <u>my friend</u>, and Isabelle, <u>my sister</u>, will be there tonight.

Apply

Complete the sentences by creating an appositive that identifies or adds information about the underlined nouns.

1. <u>Ronald and Alexander</u>, _____, always rode their bicycles to school.
   Possible Answer my neighbors

2. I read my favorite <u>book</u>, _____, again last night.
   Possible Answer *Island of the Blue Dolphins*

3. Mr. Milam had two <u>dogs</u>, _____.
   Possible Answers a Dalmatian and a poodle

4. Karen and Jim drove to my favorite <u>city</u>, _____, this weekend.
   Possible Answer Cleveland

Name _____ Date _____

Focus

An **appositive** is a noun placed next to another noun to identify it or to give more information about it.

An **appositive phrase** is an appositive and its modifiers.

Practice

Underline the appositive or appositive phrase in each sentence.

1. My teacher, <u>Mr. Samuels</u>, gives stars for good behavior.

2. Bluebell, <u>a type of wildflower</u>, blooms in the spring.

3. Thomas Edison, <u>the famous inventor</u>, lived in New Jersey.

4. Delaware, <u>the second-smallest state</u>, has only three counties.

Apply

Use an appositive or an appositive phrase to combine each pair of sentences.

1. Frisky always sleeps on my bed. Frisky is my cat.

   My cat, Frisky, always sleeps on my bed.

2. Sacramento is the capital of California. Sacramento was founded in 1848.

   Sacramento, the capital of California, was founded in 1848.

3. Kathy's father is a chef. He works in a French restaurant.

   Kathy's father, a chef, works in a French restaurant.

4. Abraham Lincoln was our sixteenth president. He was born in Kentucky.

   Abraham Lincoln, our sixteenth president, was born in Kentucky.

Name _____ Date _____

Focus

All the verbs in a sentence should have **consistent tenses** or an appropriate shift in tenses.

Practice

Underline the verbs in each sentence. Identify the tense of each verb. Then write if the tenses are consistent or not consistent.

1. I will finish my homework, and then I will play.

   future tense, future tense, consistent

2. Annie draws a house and colored it blue.

   present, past, not consistent

Apply

Rewrite each sentence so that it has consistent verb tenses.
Possible Answers

1. I always brushed my teeth after I eat breakfast.

   I always brush my teeth after I eat breakfast.

2. Calvin runs two miles and did twenty sit-ups.

   Calvin ran two miles and did twenty sit-ups.

3. Tomorrow we had a picnic, and then we will go for a hike.

   Tomorrow we will have a picnic, and then we will go for a hike.

4. Metta will work during the day and goes to school at night.

   Metta works during the day and goes to school at night.

Name _____ Date _____

Focus

A **simple sentence** has one independent clause.
A **compound sentence** has two independent clauses joined by a coordinating conjunction.
A **complex sentence** has one independent clause and at least one dependent clause.
A **compound-complex sentence** is a compound sentence and a complex sentence joined by a coordinating conjunction.

Practice

Identify the structure of each sentence from the list above.

1. He invited me to the party.   _____simple_____

2. He invited me to the party,   _____compound_____
   but I don't want to go.

3. Although he invited me to the   _____complex_____
   party, I don't want to go.

4. Although he invited me to the party, I don't   _compound-complex_
   want to go because I have other plans.

Apply

Identify the structure of each sentence from the list above.

1. The team cheered, and the fans applauded   _compound-complex_
   because our school won the championship.

2. The snow melts quickly in the sun.   _____simple_____

3. Randy sold his car, and Aleesha bought it.   _____compound_____

4. Unless we work all night, we will never finish   _____complex_____
   this job.

Name _____ **Date** _____

Focus

Quotation marks are used for dialogue and titles.
Punctuation goes inside quotation marks in all dialogue and in all titles that end in a question mark or an exclamation point.
Parentheses are used for unimportant information, abbreviations, acronyms, numbers, and around a sentence inside a sentence.
Punctuation goes inside parentheses when the words inside form a complete sentence or require a question mark or exclamation point.

Practice

Write the missing quotation marks or parentheses in each sentence.

1. My mom always says,"It is better to save than to spend."

2. The Parent Teacher Association(PTA)is having another fundraiser.

3. "Don't look down!"the guide shouted.

4. We went to Texas(What a huge state!)last year.

Apply

Rewrite each sentence with correct punctuation.

1. "I can't take this anymore"! she screamed.

   "I can't take this anymore!" she screamed.

2. We saw Jake, Allen (Jake's brother,) and Kimberly at the movies.

   We saw Jake, Allen (Jake's brother), and Kimberly at the movies.

3. Well", she said, "you sure took a long time to get here".

   "Well," she said, "you sure took a long time to get here."

Name ———————————————————— **Date** ——————————

Focus

An **appositive** is a noun placed next to another noun to identify it or to give more information about it.

An **appositive phrase** is an appositive and its modifiers.

Practice

Underline the appositive or appositive phrase in each sentence.

1. Our national tree, <u>the oak</u>, is a symbol of strength.

2. The gecko, <u>a type of lizard</u>, lives in warm climates.

3. She made tortillas, <u>a popular food in Mexico</u>.

4. My neighbor's dog, <u>Charlie</u>, likes to play catch.

Apply

Use an appositive or an appositive phrase to combine each pair of sentences. Write the sentences on the lines below.

1. Thomas Jefferson was our third president. He was born in Virginia.

   Thomas Jefferson, our third president, was born in Virginia.

2. The cheetah is the world's fastest animal. Cheetahs live in Africa.

   The cheetah, the world's fastest animal, lives in Africa.

3. Lead is a soft and heavy metal. Lead has many uses.

   Lead, a soft and heavy metal, has many uses.

4. Tanya plays the guitar. The guitar is my favorite instrument.

   Tanya plays the guitar, my favorite instrument.

Name _____ **Date** _____

Focus

Contractions are shortened forms of two words joined by an apostrophe.
Homophones are words that sound the same, but have different
meanings and spellings. Some contractions are homophones.

Practice

Circle each contraction. Then name a homophone for that contraction.

1. I hope (he'll) call back tomorrow. __heal, heel_____

2. (They're) going to a movie at noon. __there, their_____

3. (We'll) deal with that problem later. __wheel_____

4. You talk sometimes when (you're) sleeping. __your, yore_____

5. (It's) not important whether you win or lose. __its_____

Apply

Choose the correct homophone to complete each sentence.

1. ___We've___ heard so much about you.
   a. We've   **b.** Weave

2. I think ___he'll___ be a good leader.
   a. he'll   **b.** heel

3. ___He'd___ rather be playing soccer.
   a. He'd   **b.** Heed

4. We need to decide ___who's___ going to represent us.
   a. whose   **b.** who's

5. ___Their___ flight arrives tomorrow morning.
   a. They're   **b.** Their

Name _____ Date _____

Focus

A **negative sentence** tells what something or someone is not, does not have, or does not do. The adverb *not* is the most common negative word. Other negative words include *never, nobody,* and *nothing.*

Practice

Circle the negative word in each sentence.

1. He does (not) know the answer.

2. My dad (never) listens to good music.

3. (Nobody) tells me what to do.

4. There is (nothing) fun to do here.

Apply

Rewrite each positive sentence so that it is negative.

1. I bought something for you.

   I bought nothing for you. OR I did not buy something for you.

2. Everyone has finished reading the story.

   No one has finished reading the story.

3. Anybody could do this job.

   Nobody could do this job.

4. Angela always sits in the same seat.

   Angela never sits in the same seat.

Name _____ **Date** _____

Focus

Homophones are words that sound alike but have different meanings. Examples include *they're, there, their; to, two, too; it's, its*.

Practice

Underline the homophones in the following sentences.

1. Olivia bought <u>two</u> more tickets, so Matthew and Ethan could come <u>too</u>.

2. My grandparents are driving separately, so <u>they're</u> going to meet us <u>there</u>.

3. <u>It's</u> exciting to watch the animals at the zoo, especially when the bear feeds <u>its</u> cub.

4. Jordan carried <u>their</u> bags to the car parked over <u>there</u>.

Apply

Circle the correct homophones to complete the sentences below.

1. Jackson gave the lettuce (for), four) the salad (to), two) Kirk.

2. The twins had (their), there) birthday party (their, there)).

3. The parrot learned how (two, to) open the door on (its), it's) cage.

4. (They're), Their) moving three miles down the road from me.

Name _____   Date _____

Focus

A **double negative** is a sentence with two negative words.
The two main ways to correct a double negative are to remove one of the negative words or to replace one of the negative words with a positive word.

Practice

Circle the negative words in each double negative sentence.

1. She will (not) answer (no) questions.

2. I (don't) have (nothing.)

3. He (never) talks to (nobody.)

4. I (hardly) go (nowhere.)

Apply

Correct the double negative in each sentence.

1. They aren't talking to nobody.

   They aren't talking to anybody. OR They are talking to nobody.

2. She never does no homework.

   She never does any homework. OR She does no homework.

3. The driver could not find nowhere to stop.

   The driver could not find anywhere to stop. OR The driver could find nowhere to stop.

4. I don't let nothing bother me.

   I don't let anything bother me. OR I let nothing bother me.

Name _____ **Date** _____

Focus

A **participial phrase** is a group of words that begins with a participle and modifies a noun or a pronoun.

Practice

Underline the participial phrase in each sentence. Then circle the participle in the phrase.

1. (Listening) to music, Emily did not hear the doorbell.

2. We cheered for the cars (racing) down the track.

3. She caught the cat (playing) with her yarn.

4. (Frozen) in the headlights, the deer was too afraid to move.

5. The shelves are full of books (arranged) in neat rows.

Apply

Underline the participial phrase in each sentence. Then identify the noun that the phrase modifies on the line below the sentence.

1. We watched the spider spinning its web. _____ spider _____

2. Burning with a fever, Tim did not go to school. _____ Tim _____

3. Maya laughed at the monkey dressed like a clown. _____ monkey _____

4. Radiating confidence, the player walked onto the court. _____ player _____

5. He kept his bike covered with stickers. _____ bike _____

Name _____ Date _____

Focus

You can combine two sentences by placing some of the information in a **participial phrase**. Remember a **participial** is a verb form used as an adjective. Most participles end in *-ing, -ed,* or *-en.*

Practice

Underline the participial phrase in the third sentence.

1. Erica was frozen with fear. She could not speak.
   Frozen with fear, Erica could not speak.

2. The students were talking loudly. They did not hear the bell ring.
   Talking loudly, the students did not hear the bell ring.

3. My car was loaded with heavy boxes. It barely made it up the hill.
   Loaded with heavy boxes, my car barely made it up the hill.

Apply

Use a participial phrase to combine each pair of sentences.

1. Marvin was running out of gas. He searched for a gas station.

   Running out of gas, Marvin searched for a gas station.

2. Annie was shaken from the fall. She needed to rest.

   Shaken from the fall, Annie needed to rest.

3. Mrs. Brown waved to the gardener. He was mowing the grass.

   Mrs. Brown waved to the gardener mowing the grass.

4. The house was destroyed by a fire. It was never rebuilt.

   Destroyed by a fire, the house was never rebuilt.

Name _____ Date _____

Focus

Pronouns are words that replace nouns in a sentence.
Pronouns that replace subject nouns include: *I, he, she, it, you, we, they.*
Pronouns that replace object nouns include: *me, him, her, it, you, us, them.*

Practice

Circle the pronoun in each sentence. Specify if it is a replacement for a subject noun or an object noun.

1. My grandmother gave (me) an awesome present. _____ object

2. (They) won four out of five of the games. _____ subject

3. (We) moved here about five years ago. _____ subject

4. The teacher told (you) to stand in line. _____ object

5. (She) drove all the way from New York to Chicago. _____ subject

Apply

Replace the underlined words in each sentence with an appropriate pronoun.

1. Lisa is a good athlete. _____ She

2. The photographer took several pictures of Joe and me. _____ us

3. Nancy bought the tomatoes at the farmers market. _____ them

4. Mr. Randall greeted his guests at the door. _____ He

5. The scientist studied the slide under a microscope. _____ it

Name _____ Date _____

Focus
Use suffixes to change all one-syllable and some two-syllable adjectives and adverbs to their comparative and superlative forms.
Use the -er suffix to form **comparatives.**
Use the -est suffix to form **superlatives.**

Practice
Complete the chart by writing the comparative and superlative form of each adjective or adverb.

	Adjective/Adverb	Comparative	Superlative
1.	poor	poorer	poorest
2.	scary	scarier	scariest
3.	slow	slower	slowest
4.	light	lighter	lightest
5.	noisy	noisier	noisiest

Apply
Choose the best adjective or adverb to complete each sentence.

1. Your hair is _____ than mine.
   a. longer   **b.** longest

2. That was the _____ show I've ever seen!
   a. funnier   **b.** funniest

3. Of all the puppies in the litter, this one is the _____.
   a. cuter   **b.** cutest

4. You have the _____ yard in the neighborhood.
   a. nicer   **b.** nicest

Name _____ **Date** _____

Focus

For all adjectives and adverbs that have more than two syllables and some that have two syllables:
Use the word more to form **comparatives.**
Use the word most to form **superlatives.**

Practice

Complete the chart by writing the comparative and superlative form of each adjective or adverb.

	Adjective/Adverb	Comparative	Superlative
1.	difficult	more difficult	most difficult
2.	careful	more careful	most careful
3.	afraid	more afraid	most afraid
4.	successful	more successful	most successful
5.	important	more important	most important

Apply

Choose the best adjective or adverb to complete each sentence.

1. This is the _____ book I have ever read.
   a. more interesting   **b.** most interesting

2. Our new house is _____ than our old one.
   a. more modern   **b.** most modern

3. Of all the students, I think I am the _____.
   a. more confused   **b.** most confused

4. She is _____ than she needs to be.
   a. more worried   **b.** most worried